D1096569

$ **From New York** Total units ______ at $9.95 each Total amount enclosed $ ______ (N.Y. residents add sales tax)	£ **From London** Total units ______ at £5.95 Total amount enclosed £ ______ (VAT is included)

Name ______________________________

____

Address ______________________________

____

____

Please complete and return this order form to:

Traveller's Shopping Service 3490 Lawson Blvd. Oceanside, N.Y. 11572 U.S.A.	or	Traveller's Shopping Service 8, Trident Way Brent Road Southall Middlesex UB2 5LS England

Please order Berlitz books through your bookseller. Shoul[d] you encounter any difficulties, write directly to any of th[e] distributors listed on the back cover.

1140[5]

BERLITZ®

JAPANESE
FOR TRAVELLERS

By the staff of Editions Berlitz

Library of Congress Catalog Card Number: 73-2275

12th printing 1983

Printed in Switzerland

Editions Berlitz
1, avenue des Jordils
1000 Lausanne 6, Switzerland

reface

ou are about to visit Japan. Our aim is to give you a practical ırase book to help you on your trip.

ıpanese for Travellers provides:

- all the phrases and supplementary vocabulary you will need on your trip
- a wide variety of tourist and travel facts, tips and useful information
- a complete phonetic transcription, showing you the pronunciation of all the words and phrases listed
- special sections showing the replies your listener might give to you. Just hand him the book and let him point to the appropriate phrase. This is especially practical in certain difficult situations (doctor, car mechanic, etc.). It makes direct, quick and sure communication possible
- a logical system of presentation so that you can find the right phrase for the immediate situation
- quick reference through colour coding. The major features of the contents are on the back cover; a complete index is given inside.

hese are just a few of the practical advantages. In addition, the ook will prove a valuable introduction to life in Japan.

here is a comprehensive section on Eating Out, giving transıtions and explanations for practically anything one would nd on a menu in Japan; there is a complete Shopping Guide ıat will enable you to obtain virtually anything you want.

Trouble with the car? Turn to the mechanic's manual with i dual-language instructions. Feeling ill? Our medical sectio provides the most rapid communication possible between yo and the doctor.

To make the most of *Japanese for Travellers,* we suggest th you start with the "Guide to Pronunciation". Then go on "Some Basic Expressions". This not only gives you a minimu vocabulary; it helps you to pronounce the language.

We are particularly grateful to Miss Yoko Ichikawa, Mr. Hidea Dodo, Mr. Henri Takahashi and Mr. Iwao Yanagidani f their help in the preparation of this book, and also to D T.J.A. Bennett for his advice concerning the transliteration. W also wish to thank Japan Air Lines for their assistance.

We shall be very pleased to receive any comments, criticis and suggestions that you think may help us in preparing futu editions.

Thank you. Have a good trip.

Guide to pronunciation

As a minimum vocabulary for your trip, we have selected a number of basic words and phrases under the title "Some basic expressions" (pages 9–14).

An outline of the sounds of Japanese

If you follow carefully the indications supplied below, you will have no difficulty in reading the transliterations in such a way as to make yourself understood. In addition, listening to the native speakers on the record and constant practice will help you to improve your accent. (This book also contains the Japanese script. If, despite your efforts, your listener does not seem to understand you, then show him or her the book and indicate what you mean to say.)

Japanese is composed less of vowels and consonants than of syllables, consisting of a consonant and a vowel. We have decided to use a transliteration based on the Hepburn Romanisation, as this is the most helpful of the systems in use at present.

A transliteration is a representation of the sounds of the language in the Latin (our) alphabet, as opposed to the traditional Japanese alphabet. It can be read quite easily once a few rules have been mastered. The sounds represented by the transliteration are as follows:

Vowels

Letter	Approximate prounciation
a	like the vowel in c**a**r, but pronounced further forward in the mouth; or like the vowel in the French word ch**a**t
e	like **e** in t**e**n

i	like **ee** in b**ee**t
o	similar to **o** in g**o**ne but with lips slightly more rounded
u	similar to **u** in p**u**t but with lips not rounded

Consonants

These are pronounced approximately as in English with the following exceptions:

g	is pronounced as in English **g**o when at the beginning of a word; everywhere else (including in the particle **ga**) it is pronounced like the **ng** in ri**ng**
n	as in English **n**o; but when it is at the end of a word or syllable, more like **ng** in si**ng**, although it is not incorrect, even then, to pronounce it as in **no**
r	is pronounced with the tongue more or less in the position for **l** (there is no separate **l** in Japanese), but the tongue does not touch the front of the mouth, nor is the sound "rolled"
s	is always hard as in **s**ee
w	the lips are not rounded but left slack

Vowels carrying a bar, e.g., **ā, ō, ī, ū,** in our transliteration should be pronounced long. The length of vowels in Japanese is important; so you should clearly distinguish short from long vowels, as this difference can change the meaning of a word, e.g., **obasan** means aunt and **obāsan** means grandmother.

In Japanese, it should be noted, there is no strong stress except for emphasis. All syllables are pronounced with almost equal force.

ome basic expressions

s.	はい。	hai
.	いいえ。	īe
ase.	どうぞ。	dōzo
ank you.	ありがとう。	arigatō
ank you very much.	どうもありがとう。	dōmo arigatō
at's all right.	どういたしまして。	dō itashimashite

reetings

od morning.	お早ようございます。	ohayō gozaimasu
od afternoon.	今日は。	kon-nichiwa
od evening.	今晩は。	konbanwa
od night.	お休みなさい。	oyasumi nasai
od-bye.	さようなら。	sayōnara
e you later.	では又後程。	dewa mata nochi hodo
is is Mr...	こちらは…さんです。	kochira wa. . . san desu
is is Mrs...	こちらは…さんです。	kochira wa. . . san desu
is is Miss...	こちらは…さんです。	kochira wa. . . san desu

Between voiceless consonants (k, p, s, t, h) or after a voiceless consonant at the end of a phrase, the vowels **i** and **u** are generally whispered, or not pronounced at all, e.g., **mimasu** is pronounced **mimas** and **imashita** is pronounced **imashta.**

I'm very pleased to meet you.	始めましてどうぞよろしく。	hajimemashite dōzo yoroshiku
How are you?	お元気ですか。	o-genki desu ka
Very well, thank you.	ええ，お陰様で。	ē. o-kage sama de
And you?	貴方は。	anata-wa
Fine.	元気です。	genki desu
Excuse me.	失礼します。	shitsurei shimasu

Questions

Where?	どこ	doko
Where is...?	…はどこですか。	. . . wa doko desu ka
Where are...?	…はどこですか。	. . . wa doko desu ka
When?	いつ	itsu
What?	何	nani
How?	どうして／どうやって／どれ位	dōshite/dōyatte/ dore kurai
How much?	どれほど／いくら	dorehodo/ikura
How many?	いくつ／いくら	ikutsu/ikura
Who?	誰	dare
Why?	何故／どうして	naze/dōshite
Which?	どちら	dochira
What do you call this?	これは何と言いますか。	kore wa nanto iimasu ka
What do you call that?	あれは何と言いますか。	are wa nanto iimasu ka
What does this mean?	これはどう言う意味ですか。	kore wa dō yū imi desu k
What does that mean?	あれはどう言う意味ですか。	are wa dō yū imi desu ka

Do you speak... ?

Do you speak English?	英語を話しますか。	eigo o hanashimasu ka
Do you speak German?	ドイツ語を話しますか。	doitsugo o hanashimasu ka
Do you speak French?	フランス語を話しますか。	furansugo o hanashimasu ka
Do you speak Spanish?	スペイン語を話しますか。	supeingo o hanashimasu ka
Do you speak Italian?	イタリア語を話しますか。	itariago o hanashimasu ka
Could you speak more slowly, please?	もっとゆっくり話して下さい。	motto yukkuri hanashite kudasai
Please point to the phrase in the book.	この本の中から文を選んで指差して下さい。	kono hon no naka kara bun o erande yubisashite kudasai
Just a minute. I'll see if I can find it in this book.	ちょっと待って下さい。この本にあるかどうか調べて見ます。	chotto matte kudasai. kono hon ni aruka dōka shirabete mimasu
I understand.	分かりました。	wakarimashita
I don't understand.	分かりません。	wakarimasen

Can... ?

Can I have... ?	…を下さいますか。	... o kudasaimasu ka
Can we have... ?	…を下さいますか。	... o kudasaimasu ka
Can you show me... ?	…を見せて下さいますか。	... o misete kudasaimasu ka
Can you tell me... ?	…を教えて下さいますか。	... o oshiete kudasaimasu ka
Can you help me, please?	手伝って下さいますか。	tetsudatte kudasaimasu ka

Wanting

I'd like...	…が欲しいのですが。	... ga hoshii no desu ga
We'd like...	…が欲しいのですが。	... ga hoshii no desu ga
Please give me...	…を下さい。	... o kudasai
Give it to me, please.	それを下さい。	sore o kudasai
Please bring me...	…を持って来て下さい。	... o motte kite kudasai
Bring it to me, please.	それを持って来て下さい。	sore o motte kite kudasai
I'm hungry.	お腹がすきました。	onaka ga suki mashita
I'm thirsty.	喉がかわきました。	nodo ga kawaki mashita
I'm tired.	疲れました。	tsukaremashita
I'm lost.	道に迷いました。	michi ni mayoimashita
It's important.	大切です。	taisetsu desu
It's urgent.	急用です。	kyūyō desu
Hurry up!	急いで下さい。	isoide kudasai

It is/There is...

It is/It's...	…です。	... desu
Is it... ?	…ですか。	... desu ka
It isn't...	…ではありません。	... de wa arimasen
There is/There are...	…があります。	... ga arimasu
Is there/Are there... ?	…がありますか。	... ga arimasu ka
There isn't/There aren't...	…はありません。	... wa arimasen
There isn't any/There aren't any.	全然ありません。	zenzen arimasen

׀ few common words

ig/small	大きい／小さい	ōkii/chiisai
uick/slow	速い／遅い	hayai/osoi
arly/late	早い／遅い	hayai/osoi
heap/expensive	安い／高い	yasui/takai
ear/far	近い／遠い	chikai/tōi
ot/cold	暑い／冷たい（寒い）	atsui/tsumetai (samui)
ıll/empty	いっぱい／から	ippai/kara
asy/difficult	優しい／難しい	yasashii/muzukashii
eavy/light	重い／軽い	omoi/karui
pen/shut	空いている／閉まっている	aite iru/shimatte iru
ight/wrong	正しい／間違っている	tadashii/machigatte iru
ıld/new	古い／新しい	furui/atarashii
ıld/young	年とっている／若い	toshitotte iru/wakai
eautiful/ugly	きれい／みにくい	kirei/minikui
ood/bad	良い／悪い	yoi/warui
etter/worse	より良い／より悪い	yori yoi/yori warui

A few prepositions and some more useful words

at	に	ni
on	の上に	no ue ni
n	の中に	no naka ni
to	へ	e. . .
from	から	kara
nside	の中に	no naka ni
outside	の外に	no soto ni
up	上に	ue ni
down	下に	shita ni

before	の前に	no mae ni
after	の後に	no ushiro ni
with	と	to
without	なしに	nash ni
through	を通って	o tōtte
towards	に向って	ni mukatte
until	にまで	ni made
during	の間	no aida
and	と	to
or	あるいは	aruiwa
not	ない	nai
nothing	何もない	nani mo nai
none	ひとつもない	hitotsu mo nai
very	大変	taihen
also	も又	mo mata
soon	すぐに	suguni
perhaps	多分	tabun
here	ここ	koko
there	あちら	achira
now	今	ima
then	その時	sono toki

A very basic grammar

Explaining the basic principles of such an intricate and subtle language as Japanese is not an easy matter. The difference between English and Japanese is nothing like the difference between, take French and English. The pattern we are used to, that of differences in conjugations and declensions, vocabulary and idioms, is one that is limited to our group of Western languages. As soon as one sets out to compare English and an Oriental language, the difference is much more profound. Moreover, Japanese has the particularity of being practically unrelated even to any other Oriental language.

Generally speaking, a foreign language not only implies different words and sentence constructions, but also a different way of thinking and reasoning. This is all the more true for Japan. The country, the people, their customs and above all their language have been almost totally isolated for over 2000 years. The result is a totally different way of experiencing life.

Japanese has a limited affinity with Chinese: they are related in writing and, to a certain extent, in vocabulary. The Japanese have adopted a great number of Chinese words and characters. These often have a polite, scientific or cultural bearing, in the same way as words of French (Latin) origin in English have a more lofty meaning than those of Anglo-Saxon origin. They are not normally those used in everyday language by the man in the street. Also, Japanese is undergoing steady change and is developing as time goes on. Words and characters disappear and new ones are picked up, just like our English is no longer that of Shakespeare's day.

Japanese has a certain number of dialects; someone from the north of the country may be incapable of understanding a man from the south. However, when they get together they will generally make themselves understood by using the dialect of Tokyo which is accepted as being the leading version of Japanese.

A sentence in the making

The few grammatical notes below do not account for the psychology of Japanese speech. You'll just have to keep in mind that it is virtually unconceivable to substitute or translate a Japanese phrase by an English counterpart. Here we are only concerned with the grammatical structure, the architecture of a Japanese sentence.

The basic word order in Japanese is subject—object—verb. This is a rather rigid rule: the verb always comes last in a sentence. Subordinate clauses always precede the main clause. Here's an example to illustrate those two facts. Where a speaker of English would say:

My wife wore a new dress when she came home,

a speaker of Japanese will turn the parts of speech around and say:

My wife home came when, she a new dress wore.

Also, English tends to stress syllables within words and words within phrases. In our example, the words "wife", "dress" and "home" would probably carry more emphasis than the others. In Japanese, however, stress is highly regular and monotone. All syllables and words are pronounced with almost equal force in a staccato way.

Nouns and adjectives

Japanese nouns have no articles. Plurals do not exist either. Thus, the word **hon** may mean book, the book, a book, books or the books. All nouns have one single form which does not change according to the noun's role in the sentence.

Japanese adjectives, in turn, are very different from their English counterparts. They have tenses and moods as if they were verbs. The true Japanese adjective is an adjective with a sense of "to e" attached to it. An improvised rendition of "a new dress" in apanese could be "a new-being dress". The past tense of these djectives is formed by adding **katta** to their basic stem:

takai	expensive	**yasui**	cheap
takakatta	"was expensive"	**yasukatta**	"was cheap"

There are a certain number of adjectives which are formed lifferently: these are of Chinese origin. Bringing our Japanese phrase up to date, we say:

My wife home came when, she new-being dress wore.

Verbs

There is at least one field where (to a certain extent) Japanese is nuch simpler than English: verbs. The Japanese verb has only two tenses—present and past (where in most cases the ending is **ta**). A future tense does not exist but is understood from the context, just like the plurals of nouns. However, this simplicity is argely offset by the existence of numerous polite forms. These are basically the result of the sharply-defined social strata in Japan which gave birth to numerous graduations in polite speech. The way our speaker feels about the dress his wife wore, and above all the person he is speaking to, will define the grade of politeness of the verb form he'll choose. They can hardly be expressed in English. Here's an example:

taberu	to eat	**nomu**	to drink
tabemasu	to eat (polite)	**nomimasu**	to drink (polite)

Apart from politeness, a great number of other ways of feeling, moods and opinions are expressed through a complex web of verb forms.

And there is yet another difference. The verbs, apart from having only two tenses, have no special form to indicate person or number. On top of that, personal pronouns are usually omitted. They, too, are understood from the context, and the Japanese feel that they're not necessary.

What's now left of our sentence? It has started taking the shape of a Japanese sentence—pared down to its essentials. But we're not ready yet.

Particles

Subject and direct object are not understood from the word order as in English. When a noun is used as a subject, either the particle **ga** or the particle **wa** is added after it to indicate this; a noun used as a direct object takes the postposition **o.** In fact, particles are to Japanese what word order and prepositions are to English. That is also true of questions. These are not formed by inversion of verb and subject and by intonation, as in many Western languages, but again a special particle (**ka**) is added and pronounced at the end of the phrase. It's roughly an equivalent of our question mark.

My wife ga home came when, my wife wa new-being dress o wore.

By now you must be curious how a real Japanese would say that. Here it is:

妻が家に帰って来た時，妻は新しいドレスを着ていました。

tsuma ga ie ni kaette kita toki, tsuma wa atarashii doresu o kite imashita.

That's Japanese for you. If you have a close look at it and compare the Japanese characters with the transliteration and our English "translation", you're sure to discover similarities illustrating the rules we've explained above.

Those characters

It is beyond the scope of this book to go into a detailed explanation of how Japanese is written; but the following concise description will give you a basic idea which may help you to decipher some signs and put you on the right track. Traditionally, Japanese is written from top to bottom, starting in the upper *right*-hand corner. But it's also written horizontally and from left to right (as in this book). Basically, the Japanese script you'll be gazing at is a mixture of three different "spelling systems", called *kanji, hiragana* and *katakana*.

Kanji

As was mentioned before, Japanese has taken over characters and vocabulary from Chinese (although they're unrelated gramatically). These Chinese characters are called *kanji*. The Japanese government has approved a basic list of 1,850 of them, but there are many more. One dictionary even gives some 50,000! *Kanji* are symbols for concepts: 1 word = 1 character, as opposed to *hiragana* and *katakana,* which represent syllables. *Kanji* characters may consist of as many as 33 different strokes, but many of them have been simplified since World War II.

Hiragana

There are 46 *hiragana* characters. These are used for writing authentically Japanese words, and often also for particles and endings of words spelled in *kanji*. These characters can be recognised by their flowing, round form.

Katakana

This is a kind of shorthand, more angular than *hiragana*. It is often used for writing English and other foreign words and names in Japanese. All characters of *hiragana* and *katakana* represent one syllable. *Katakana* has five groups of syllables based on the vowels used. Here they are:

ア a	カ ka	サ sa	タ ta	ナ na	ハ ha	マ ma	ヤ ya	ラ ra	ワ wa
イ i	キ ki	シ shi	チ chi	ニ ni	ヒ hi	ミ mi		リ ri	
ウ u	ク ku	ス su	ツ tsu	ヌ nu	フ fu	ム mu	ユ yu	ル ru	
エ e	ケ ke	セ se	テ te	ネ ne	ヘ he	メ me		レ re	
オ o	コ ko	ソ so	ト to	ノ no	ホ ho	モ mo	ヨ yo	ロ ro	ヲ (w)o
				ン n					

アメリカ
(a-me-ri-ka)
America

ニホン
(ni-ho-n)
Japan

Arrival

You've arrived. Whether you've come by ship or plane, you'l have to go through passport and customs formalities.

There's certain to be somebody around who speaks English That's why we're making this a brief section. What you want i to be off to your hotel or on your way in the shortest possibl time. Here are the stages for a speedy departure.

Passport Control

In these days of the jumbo jet, you may well be waved througl passport control with a smile. Otherwise:

Here's my passport.	これが私のパスポートです。	kore ga watashi no pasupōto desu
I'll be staying . . .	…滞在の予定です。	. . . taizai no yotei desu
a few days	二,三日	ni-san nichi
a week	一週間	isshū-kan
two weeks	二週間	ni-shū-kan
a month	一ケ月	ikkagetsu
I don't know yet.	まだ分かりません。	mada wakarimasen
I'm here on holiday.	休暇で来ています。	kyuka de kite imasu
I'm here on business.	仕事で来ています。	shigoto de kite imasu
I'm just passing through.	ちょっと立ち寄るだけです。	chotto tachiyoru dake desu

If things become difficult:

I'm sorry, I don't understand. Is there anyone here who speaks English?	ごめんなさい。分かりません。ここに英語を話す人がいますか。	gomen nasai. wakarimasen. koko ni eigo o hanasu hito ga imasu ka

Customs

Believe it or not, the customs officials are just as eager to wave ou through as you are to go.

'he chart below shows you what you can bring in duty-free.*

Cigarettes		Cigars		Tobacco	Liquor (spirits)		Wine
400	or	100	or	500 grams	3	or	3

At major airports, Japan has adopted what is becoming a customs-clearance practice in many countries. A few arriving ravellers are spot-checked. Otherwise, baggage isn't even opened. After collecting your luggage, you will have to choose one of hree ways out: one is marked with a green sign, another with red sign, and the third is white and carries the words "non-esidents". This will probably have to be your choice. There you nay need to say:

have nothing to declare.	申告する物は何もありません。	shinkoku suru mono wa nani mo arimasen
have . . .	…持っています。	. . . motte imasu
400 cigarettes	たばこを 400本	tabako o yonhyappon
a bottle of whisky	ウィスキーを一本	uisukī o ippon
a bottle of wine	ブドー酒を一本	budōshu o ippon
Must I pay on this?	税金を払わなくてはいけませんか。	zeikin o harawanakutewa ikemasen ka
How much?	いくらですか。	ikura desu ka
It's for my personal use/It's not new.	それは私が使う物です／新品ではありません。	sore wa watashi ga tsukau mono desu/shinpin de wa arimasen

All allowances subject to change without notice and measures approximate. Although ustoms officers hardly ever quibble about the difference between a litre bottle and a quart ottle, they do have the right to be literal if they choose.

Possible answers

税金を払わなくてはいけませんよ。	You'll have to pay duty on this.
あそこの窓口で払って下さい。	Please pay at the office over there.
荷物はもっとありますか。	Have you any more luggage?

Baggage—Porters

The porter may take your bags to customs for you. He will then wait till they have been cleared. Note the number on his badge

Porter!	ポーター(赤帽)さん。	pōtā san
Can you help me with my luggage?	荷物を運んで下さい。	nimotsu o hakonde kudasai
That's mine.	それは私のです。	sore wa watashi no desu
That's my . . .	それは私の…です。	sore wa watashi no . . . desu
bag/luggage/suitcase	バッグ/手荷物/かばん	baggu/tenimotsu/kaban
That . . . one.	あの…の。	ano . . . no
big/small	大きい/小さい	ōkii/chiisai
blue/brown/black	青い/茶色/黒い	aoi/chairo/kuroi
There's one missing.	ひとつ見当りません。	hitotsu miatarimasen
Take these bags to the . . .	このバッグを…へ持って行って下さい。	kono baggu o . . . e motte itte kudasai
taxi/bus/luggage lockers	タクシー/バス/荷物預り所	takushī/basu/nimotsu-azukarijo
Get me a taxi, please.	タクシーを呼んで下さい。	takushī o yonde kudasai
Where's the bus for the air terminal?	空港ターミナルへ行くバスはどこから出ますか。	kūkōtāminaru e yuku basu wa doko kara demasu ka
How much is that?	いくらですか。	ikura desu ka

Note: The normal rate is about 200 yen per bag. Have some small change ready.

Changing money

Foreign currency and traveller's cheques (checks) can be exchanged or cashed only at authorized exchange offices. Most hotel exchange counters stay open in the evening, and the airport bank is open 24 hours. Personal cheques are not usually accepted. Remember to bring along your passport, since you may need it. For more detailed information, see pages 134–136.

Where's the nearest currency exchange?	最寄りの両替所はどこですか。	moyori no ryōgaejo wa doko desu ka
Can you change a traveller's cheque (check)?	トラベラーチェックを両替出来ますか。	toraberā cheku o ryōgae dekimasu ka
I want to change some . . .	…を両替したいのですが。	. . . o ryōgae shitai no desu ga
traveller's cheques	トラベラーチェック	toraberā cheku
dollars	ドル	doru
pounds	ポンド	pondo

Directions

How do I get to . . . . . . ?	…にはどう行ったらいいでしょうか。	. . . ni wa dō ittara iideshō ka
Is there a bus into town?	市内へ行くバスはありますか。	shinai e yuku basu wa arimasu ka
Where can I get a taxi?	どこでタクシーに乗れますか。	doko de takushī ni noremasu ka
Where can I rent a car?	車はどこで借りられますか。	kuruma wa doko de kariraremasu ka

Hotel reservations

Obviously, it is safest to book in advance if you can. But if you haven't done so?

The Japan Travel Bureau (*kōtsūkōsha*) can help you. There is a JTB office open 24 hours a day in the main hall at Tokyo International Airport. You will certainly find someone there who speaks English.

FOR NUMBERS, see page 175

Car rental

Again, it's best to make arrangements in advance whenever possible. There are car rental firms in major cities. You are almost certain to find someone there who speaks English. But if nobody does, try one of the following. . .

I'd like . . .	…を借りたいのですが。	. . . o karitai no desu ga
a car	車	kuruma
a small car	小型車	kogatasha
a large car	大型車	ōgatasha
a sports car	スポーツカー	supōtsu kā
I would like it for . . .	…借りたいのですが。	. . . karitai no desu ga
a day/four days	一日/四日間	ichi-nichi/yokka-kan
a week/two weeks	一週間/二週間	isshū-kan/ni-shū-kan
What's the charge per day?	一日の料金はいくらですか。	ichi-nichi no ryōkin wa ikura desu ka
What's the charge per week?	一週間の料金はいくらですか。	isshū-kan no ryōkin wa ikura desu ka
Does that include mileage?	マイル数（キロ数）も入っていますか。	mairu sū (kiro sū) mo haitte imasu ka
Is petrol (gasoline) included?	ガソリン代も入っていますか。	gasorindai mo haitte imasu ka
Does that include full insurance?	保険は全部入っていますか。	hoken wa zenbu haitte imasu ka
What's the deposit?	保証金はいくらですか。	hoshōkin wa ikura desu ka
I have a credit card.	クレジットカードを持っています。	kurejitto kādo o motte imasu
Here's my driving licence.	私の運転免許証です。	watashi no untenmenkyoshō desu

Note: An International Driving Licence is mandatory except for holders of U.S. and Canadian driving licences.

FOR SIGHTSEEING, see page 75

Taxi

All taxis have meters. It is usually best to ask the approximate fare beforehand. From 11 p.m. to 7 a.m. there is a supplementary fare, which is indicated on the meter. No tip is required. Nearly all taxis in Japan have automatic doors, which means that you don't close them yourself.

Where can I get a taxi?	どこでタクシーに乗れますか。	doko de takushī ni noremasu ka
Get me a taxi, please.	タクシーを呼んで下さい。	akushī o yonde kudasai
What's the fare to . . . ?	…までいくらですか。	. . . made ikura desu ka
How far is it to . . . ?	…までどの位ありますか。	. . . made dono kurai arimasu ka
Take me to . . .	…に連れて行って下さい。	. . . ni tsurete itte kudasai
this address	この住所	kono jūsho
the centre of town	町の中心	machi no chūshin
the . . . Hotel	…ホテル	. . . hoteru
Go straight ahead.	まっすぐに行って下さい。	massugu ni itte kudasai
Turn . . . at the next corner.	次の曲り角を…曲って下さい。	tsugi no magarikado o . . . magatte kudasai
left/right	左へ/右へ	hidari e/migi e
Stop here, please.	ここで止って下さい。	koko de tomatte kudasai
I'm in a hurry.	急いでいます。	isoide imasu
There's no hurry.	急がなくてもいいですよ。	isoganakute mo ii desu yo
Could you drive more slowly?	もう少しゆっくり運転して下さい。	mō sukoshi yukkuri unten shite kudasai

ARRIVAL

Hotel—Inn—Other accommodation

Early reservation (and confirmation) is essential in most majo tourist centres during the high season. Most towns and arriva points have a Japan Travel Bureau (*kōtsūkōsha*) office, and that' the place to go if you're stuck without a room.

In Japan, you can choose between two totally different types o hotels: Western-style and Japanese-style. The latter is generall cheaper.

Western-style hotels

In major Japanese cities and tourist resorts there are man Western-style hotels which maintain quality standards compa rable to modern hotels in Europe or the U.S. They range fron luxury class to modest hotels.

Japanese-style inns (ryokan)

Staying at a *ryokan,* besides being cheaper than staying in Western-style hotel, will enable you to sample a bit of Japanes life: Japanese atmosphere, Japanese bath, Japanese bed, etc The *ryokans* look practically the same as ordinary Japanes houses except that they are much larger, with a minimum c 11 guest rooms. You will also receive personal service and atten tion akin to the hospitality of a Japanese family. Each guest roon has its own chambermaid. Prices generally include room, dinne and breakfast.

There are currently over 70,000 *ryokans* in Japan, of whicl about 900 have facilities for handling Western visitors, such a individual bathrooms and Western-style washrooms. They ca also prepare simple Western-style meals. The overwhelmin majority of the *ryokans*, however, are not accustomed to caterin to Western guests, but, precisely for this reason, staying in on the lesser *ryokans* may be an exciting way to spend your days Japan in the real Japanese way.

you would like to see how the Japanese really live, you may range to stay with a Japanese family as a paying guest by concting Tourist Information Centres in major Japanese cities. this section, we are mainly concerned with the smaller and iddle-class hotels and inns. You'll have no language difficulties the luxury and first-class hotels where at least some of the staff ave been trained to speak English.

the next few pages we shall consider your requirements—step y step—from arrival to departure. There's no need to read through e whole lot. Just turn to the situation that applies.

hecking in—Reception

Ay name is . . .	…ですが。	. . . desu ga
have a reservation.	予約してあります。	yoyaku shite arimasu
Ve have reserved wo rooms, a single nd a double.	シングルとダブルを一部屋づつ予約してあります。	shinguru to daburu o hitoheya zutsu yoyaku shite arimasu
wrote to you last nonth. Here's the onfirmation.	先月手紙で予約しました。これがその確認です。	sengetsu tegami de yoyaku shimashita. kore ga sono kakunin desu
'd like . . .	…が欲しいのですが。	. . . ga hoshii no desu ga
single room	シングルルーム	shinguru rūmu
double room	ダブルルーム	daburu rūmu
wo single rooms	シングル二部屋	shingura futa-heya
room with twin beds	ツインベッドの部屋	tsuinbedo no heya
room with a bath	風呂付きの部屋	furotsuki no heya
room with a shower	シャワー付きの部屋	shawā tsuki no heya
a room with a balcony	バルコニー付きの部屋	barukonī tsuki no heya
a room with a view	景色の良い部屋	keshiki no yoi heya
a suite	次の間付き	tsuginoma tsuki

We'd like a room . . .	…部屋が欲しいのですが。	. . . heya ga hoshii no de ga
in the front/ at the back	表側の/ 裏側の	omotegawa no/ uragawa no
facing the sea	海に面した	umi ni menshita
facing the courtyard	中庭に面した	nakaniwa ni menshita
It must be quiet.	静かな部屋をお願いします。	shizukana heya o o-negai shimasu
I'd rather have something higher up (lower down).	上の階（下の階）を希望します。	ue no kai (shita no kai) o kibō shimasu
Is there . . . ?	…はありますか。	. . . wa arimasu ka
air conditioning/ heating	冷房/暖房	reibō/danbō
hot water/running water	お湯/水道	oyu/suidō
a laundry/valet service	洗濯/ボーイのサービス	sentaku/bōi no sābisu
a private toilet	個人用の手洗	kojin-yō no te-arai
a radio/television in the room	ラジオ/部屋にテレビ	rajio/heya ni terebi

How much?

What's the price . . ?	…の料金はいくらですか。	. . . no ryōkin wa ikura de ka
per night/per week	一泊/一週間	ippaku/isshū-kan
for bed and breakfast	朝食付き	chōshokutsuki
excluding meals	食事抜き	shokuji nuki
for full board	三食付き	sanshoku tsuki
Does that include . . . ?	…は入っていますか。	. . . wa haitte imasu ka
breakfast/meals/ service	朝食/食事/サービス	chōshoku/shokuji/sābisu
Is there any reduction for children?	子供の割引はありますか。	kodomo no waribiki wa arimasu ka

o you charge for ıe baby?	赤ん坊も勘定に入りますか。	akanbō mo kanjō ni hairimasu ka
hat's too expensive.	高過ぎます。	takasugimasu
aven't you anything heaper?	ほかにもっと安い部屋はありませんか。	hokani motto yasui heya wa arimasen ka

low long?

Ve'll be staying . . .	…滞在します。	. . . taizai shimasu
vernight only/a few days	一泊だけ/二，三日	ippaku dake/ni-san nichi
week (at least)	（少なくとも）一週間	(sukunaku tomo) isshū-kan
don't know yet.	まだ分かりません。	mada wakarimasen

)ecision

⁄lay I see the room?	部屋を見せて頂けますか。	heya o misete itadakemasu ka
lo, I don't like it.	気に入りません。	kiniirimasen
's too . . .	…過ぎます	. . . sugimasu
old/hot	寒/暑	samu/atsu
ark/small/noisy	暗/小さ/喧し	kura/chiisa/yakamashi
lo, that won't do at ll.	あれでは全然だめです。	are de wa zenzen dame desu
lave you anything . . ?	何か…のはありませんか。	nanika . . . no wa arimasen ka
etter/bigger	もっと良い/もっと大きな	motto yoi/motto ōkina
heaper/smaller	もっと安い/もっと小さい	motto yasui/motto chīsai
lave you a room with better view?	もっと景色の良い部屋がありますか。	motto keshiki no yoi heya ga arimasu ka
hat's fine. I'll take it.	これはいいですね。これにします。	kore wa iidesu ne. kore ni shimasu

OR NUMBERS, see page 176

Bills

These are usually paid weekly, or on departure if you stay les than a week. Most hotels offer a reduction for children under

Tipping

A service charge varying between 10% and 15% is normall included in the bill. But you can ask: *Sābisuryo wa haitte imasuka* (Is service included?). Tip the porter when he brings the bags t your room. Also tip the bellboy if he does any errands for yo Otherwise, however, tipping is not customary in Japan.

Registration

Upon arrival at a hotel you will be asked to fill in a registratic form. It asks your name, home address, passport number an further destination. It's almost certain to carry an English tran lation. However, if you stay in a Japanese-style hotel (*ryokan* especially in the country, they may have it only in Japanese. The you ask the chambermaid:

What does this mean?	これは何ですか。	kore wa nan desu ka

She will probably ask you for your passport. She may want keep it for a while, even overnight. Don't worry—you'll get it bac The chambermaid may want to ask you the following questions:

パスポートを見せて下さい。	May I see your passport?
このカードに記入して頂けますか。	Would you mind filling in this registration form?
ここにサインして下さい。	Sign here, please.
どの位御滞在になりますか。	How long will you be staying?

ervice, please

ow that you are safely installed, meet some more of the hotel aff:

:he bellboy	ボーイさん	bōi san
the chambermaid	メイドさん	meido san
:he manager	マネージャーさん	manējā san
:he telephone operator	電話交換手さん	denwa kōkanshu san

;eneral requirements

lease ask the hambermaid to ome up.	メイドさんに来るように言って下さい。	meido san ni kuru yō ni itte kudasai
Vho is it?	誰ですか。	dare desu ka
ust a minute.	ちょっと待って下さい。	chotto matte kudasai
:ome in.	どうぞ。	dōzo
he door's open.	ドアは開いてますよ。	doā wa aite imasu yo
s there a bath on this 'oor?	この階にはお風呂がありますか。	kono kai ni wa o-furo ga arimasu ka

Jote: If you stay in a *ryokan* (Japanese-style inn) in the country, here may be only one large bathroom available which you'll ave to share with other clients.

Iow does this ;hower work?	シャワーはどうしたら使えますか。	shawā wa dō shitara tsukae-musu ka
Vhere's the plug for shaver?	電気カミソリ用の差し込みはどこにありますか。	denkikamisori-yō no sashikomi wa doko ni arimasu ka
Vhat's the voltage?	電圧は何ボルトですか。	denatsu wa nan boruto desu ka
Please send up . . .	…を持って来て下さい。	. . . o motte kite kudasai
:wo coffees/ sandwiches/gin and tonics	コーヒー二つ/サンドウィッチ/ジントニック	kōhī futatsu/sandoittchi/ jin tonikku

Can we have breakfast in our room?	部屋で朝食をとれますか。	heya de chōshoku o tore-masu ka
I'd like to leave these in your safe.	これを金庫に預って頂きたいのですが。	kore o kinko ni azukatte itadakitai no desu ga
Can you find me a baby-sitter?	ベービイシッターをお願い出来ますか。	bebī-shitā o o-negai dekimasu ka
May I have a/an/some . . . ?	…を下さい。	. . . o kudasai
ashtray	灰皿	haizara
bath towel	バスタオル	basutaoru
extra blanket	毛布をもう一枚	mōfu o mō ichi-mai
envelopes	封筒	fūto
(more) hangers	ハンガー（をもう少し）	hangā (o mō sukoshi)
hot-water bottle	湯たんぽ	yutanpo
ice	氷	kōri
needle and thread	針と糸	hari to ito
extra pillow	枕をもう一つ	makura o mō hitotsu
reading-lamp	スタンド	sutando
soap	石けん	sekken
writing-paper	便箋	binsen
Where's the . . . ?	…はどこですか。	. . . wa doko desu ka
bathroom	風呂場	furoba
beauty parlour	美容院	biyōin
cocktail lounge	バー	bā
dining-room	食堂	shokudō
hairdresser's	床屋	tokoya
perfume shop	化粧品店	keshōhinten
restaurant	レストラン	resutoran
television room	テレビのある部屋	terebi no aru heya
toilet	手洗	te-arai

HOTEL-SERVICE

Breakfast

If you stay in a Japanese-style hotel (*ryokan*), you will automatically be served the standard Japanese breakfast consisting of a bowl of rice, soy bean soup, seaweed, raw eggs, etc. If this does not appeal to you, you may order a Western-style breakfast the night before. In cheaper *ryokans* or in *ryokans* in the country, however, it is advisable not to do so, as they may not know how to prepare a Western-style breakfast.

At Western-style hotels you'll have no problem. They provide Continental, English or American breakfasts.

I'll have a/an/some . . .	…が欲しいのですが。	. . . ga hoshii no desu ga
bacon and eggs	ベーコンと卵	bēkon to tamago
cereal	コーンフレークス	kōnfureikusu
hot/cold	熱い/冷たい	atsui/tsumetai
eggs	卵	tamago
boiled egg	ゆで卵	yude tamago
soft/medium/hard	生ゆで／半じゅく／固ゆで	namayude/hanjuku/katayude
fried	目玉焼	medama yaki
scrambled	いり卵	iri tamago
fruit juice	フルーツジュース	furūtsu jūsu
grapefruit/orange	グレープフルーツ／オレンジ	gurēpu furūtsu/orenji
pineapple/tomato	パイナップル／トマト	painappuru/tomato
ham and eggs	ハムエッグ	hamueggu
omelet	オムレツ	omuretsu
sausages	ソーセージ	sōsēji
May I have some . . . ?	…を下さい。	. . . o kudasai
hot/cold milk	熱い／冷たいミルク	atsui/tsumetai miruku
cream/sugar	クリーム／砂糖	kurīmu/satō
more butter	バターをもう少し	batā o mō sukoshi
salt/pepper	塩／胡椒	shio/kosyō
coffee/tea	コーヒー／紅茶	kōhī/kōcha
chocolate	チョコレート	chokorēto
lemon/honey	レモン／蜂蜜	remon/hachimitsu

Could you bring me a . . . ?	…を持って来て下さい。	. . . o motte kite kudasai
cup	茶碗	chawan
fork	フォーク	fōku
glass	コップ	koppu
knife	ナイフ	naifu
plate	皿	sara
spoon	スプーン	supūn

Note: You'll find a great many other dishes listed in our guid "Eating out" (pages 39–64). This should be consulted for you lunch and dinner menus.

Difficulties

The . . . doesn't work.	…がこわれています。	. . . ga kowarete imasu
air-conditioner	冷房装置	reibōsōchi
fan	扇風機	senpūki
faucet	水道の栓	suidō no sen
heating	暖房	danbō
light	電灯	dentō
tap	水道の栓	suidō no sen
toilet	手洗	te-arai
ventilator	換気装置	kankisōchi
The wash-basin is clogged.	洗面台がつまっています。	senmendai ga tsumatte imasu
The window is jammed.	窓が動きません。	mado ga ugokimasen
The blind is stuck.	ブラインドが動きません。	buraindo ga ugokimasen
These aren't my shoes.	これは私の靴ではありません。	kore wa watashi no kutsu de wa arimasen
This isn't my laundry.	これは私の洗濯物ではありません。	kore wa watashi no sentakumono de wa arimase
There's no hot water.	お湯が出ません。	oyu ga demasen
I've lost my . . .	…をなくしました。	. . . o nakushimashita
watch/key	時計／鍵	tokē/kagi

I've left my key in my room.	鍵を私の部屋に置き忘れました。	kagi o watashi no heya ni okiwasure mashita
The . . . is broken.	…がこわれています。	. . . ga kowarete imasu
bulb	電球	denkyū
lamp	ランプ	ranpu
plug	差し込み	sashikomi
shutter	よろい戸	yoroido
switch	スイッチ	suittchi
venetian blind	ブラインド	buraindo
window shade	日よけ	hiyoke
Can you get it fixed?	これを直して頂けますか。	kore o naoshite itadakemasu ka
Can you replace it?	これを取り換えて頂けますか。	kore o torikaete itadakemasu ka

Telephone—Mail—Callers

Can you get me Tokyo 123 4567?	東京 123 4567 をお願いします。	tōkyō ichi-ni-san yon-go-roku-nana o o-negai shimasu
Did anyone call me?	誰か私に電話を掛けて来ましたか。	dare ka watashi ni denwa o kakete kimashita ka
Operator, I've been cut off.	交換手さん。電話が切れてしまったのですが。	kōkanshu san, denwa ga kirete shimatta no desu ga
Is there any mail for me?	私あてに郵便物が来ていますか。	watashi ate ni yūbinbutsu ga kite imasu ka
Have you any stamps?	切手がありますか。	kitte ga arimasu ka
Would you mail this for me, please?	これを発送して頂けますか。	kore o hassō shite itadakemasu ka
Are there any messages for me?	何か私あてに言付けがありますか,	nani ka watashi ate ni kotozuke ga arimasu ka

FOR POST OFFICE, see page 137

Checking out

May I have my bill, please? Room 398.	勘定書を下さい。398号室です。	kanjōgaki o kudasai. sanbyaku kyujū hachi gō shitsu desu
I'm leaving early tomorrow. Please have my bill ready.	明日早く立ちます。勘定書を用意して置いて下さい。	asu hayaku tachimasu. kanjōgaki o yōi shite oite kudasai
We'll be checking out . . .	…チェックアウトします。	. . . cheku auto shimasu
around noon/soon	お昼頃／間もなく	ohirugoro/mamonaku
I must leave at once.	今すぐ立たなければなりません。	ima sugu tatanakereba narimasen
Does this include . . . ?	…は入っていますか。	. . . wa haitte imasu ka
service/tax	サービス料／税金	sābisuryō/zeikin
Is everything included?	全部入っていますか。	zenbu haitte imasu ka
You've made a mistake in this bill, I think.	勘定書に間違いがあるようですが。	kanjōgaki ni machigai ga aru yō desu ga
It's too high. It's ridiculous.	高過ぎます。べらぼうですね。	takasugimasu. berabō desu ne
Can you get a taxi?	タクシーを呼んで下さい。	takushi o yonde kudasai
Would you send someone to bring down our baggage?	荷物を降ろすのに誰かよこして下さい。	nimotsu o orosu no ni dareka yokoshite kudasai
We're in a great hurry.	私達は非常に急いでいます。	watashitachi wa hijō ni isoide imasu
Here's the forwarding address. You have my home address.	これが次の宛先です。私の住所は御存知ですね。	kore ga tsugi no atesaki desu. watashi no jūsho wa go-zonji desu ne
It's been a very enjoyable stay.	楽しい滞在でした。	tanoshii taizai deshita
I hope we'll come again sometime.	いつか又来ましょう。	itsuka mata kimashō

FOR TAXI, see page 27

HOTEL-SERVICE

Eating out

There are many types of eating and drinking places in Japan. Going to a restaurant in Japan is very much like going to a restaurant in the West, but there are some that specialize in dishes like *sukiyaki*, *tempura* or *sushi*; therefore, pay attention to what kind of restaurant you're entering. Also, if you want to be sure of getting good value for money, go to a *sukiyaki* restaurant if you want to try *sukiyaki* or to a *tempura* restaurant if it's *tempura* you're after. If you wish, you can reserve a private dining room (*o-zashiki*) in a Japanese-style restaurant. Having taken your shoes off at the entrance, you'll squat down on the *tatami* (rice straw mat floor).

バー *(bā)*	Bar. Drinks and snacks served. Most bars have numerous hostesses, and you'll have to pay for their drinks, too.
ビヤガーデン *(biyagāden)*	Beer garden. Beer and snacks served on the rooftops of downtown buildings.
喫茶店 *(kissaten)*	Coffee shop. This is the most prevalent phenomenon throughout Japan. Coffee, soft drinks and snacks are served. All coffee shops have music.
飲み屋 *(nomiya)*	*Sake* bar specializing in the famed Japanese rice wine, but also serving beer, appetizers and Japanese-style snacks.
レストラン *(restoran)*	1. Restaurant (foreign). In major cities like Tokyo and Osaka, you'll find restaurants of many different nationalities. 2. To be distinguished from a foreign restaurant. Serves both Japanese and Japanized Western-style food.

料理屋 *(ryoriya)*	Specialized in Japanese-style food only. Try one of these: *sukiyaki, tempura, sashimi, sushi, yakitori.* Some specialize in one of these dishes only. Basically, *ryoriya* can be divided into two categories: the *ozashiki* (private room) restaurant where the meal is served in your own Japanese-style room, and the counter restaurant where your dish will be prepared in front of you. However, some *ryoriya* will combine these two types or even have tables and chairs.
スナックバー *(sunakku-bā)*	Snack bar. The Japanese have taken over the word. In Tokyo, many of them are open all night.

Many restaurants display wax representations of their dishes together with the prices in glass cases facing the street.

Meal times

Breakfast (*chōshoku*): until 9 a.m.
Lunch (*chūshoku*): from noon to 2 p.m.
Dinner (*yūshoku*): from 6 p.m. to 9 p.m.

To get a table in a well-known restaurant, telephone in advance:

I'd like to reserve a table for four, for 8 o'clock tonight.	今夜8時に4人用のテーブルを予約したいのですが。	konya hachi-ji ni yo-nin-yō no tēburu o yoyaku shitai no desu ga

few words on Japanese table manners

ne Japanese, like the Chinese, eat with chopsticks. They were troduced into Japan from China in the 5th century together th the Chinese ideograms or characters.

ow to use chopsticks can be briefly explained as follows: you ld the upper stick between your thumb and first two fingers, hile you keep the lower stick stationary with your third finger both your second and third fingers; and you hold the sticks e third above the hand and two thirds below.

panese restaurants usually will bring you a pair of wooden lf-split chopsticks in paper envelopes. You can easily split em into two. In Japanese homes, however, permanently -usable sticks are used. Such chopsticks are nowadays some-nes made of plastic.

ne Japanese have an entirely different concept of decorum from rs when it comes to eating etiquette. For instance, it's per-ctly good form in Japan to make palatal noises while eating, hereas this is considered bad table manners in the West. In fact, panese often make such noises to show their appreciation of e quality of the food served.

Japanese-style restaurants or Japanese homes, you won't on chairs and around a high table as we do in the West. ou'll have to squat down on the *tatami* (straw mat floor). How-er, you'll not be required to sit in the Japanese way (literally ting on your folded legs).

Hungry?

I am hungry/I am thirsty.	お腹がすきました／喉がかわきました。	o-naka ga sukimashita/nod ga kawakimashita
Can you recommend a good (and inexpensive) restaurant?	良い（そして高くない）レストランを紹介して下さい。	yoi (soshite takakunai) resutoran o shōkai shite kudasai

Asking and ordering

Good evening. I'd like a table for three.	今晩は，3人用のテーブルはありますか。	konbanwa, san-nin-yō no tēburu wa arimasu ka
Could we have a . . . ?	…がいいのですが。	. . . ga ii no desu ga
table in the corner	隅のテーブル	sumi no tēburu
table by the window	窓の側のテーブル	mado no soba no tēburu
table outside	表のテーブル	omote no tēburu
table on the terrace	テラスのテーブル	terasu no tēburu
Where are the toilets?	手洗はどこですか。	te-arai wa doko desu ka
Can you serve me right away? I'm in a hurry.	急いでいますからすぐにして下さい。	isoide imasu kara sugu ni shite kudasai
What's the price of the fixed menu?	今日の定食はいくらですか。	kyō no teishoku wa ikura desu ka
Is service included?	サービス料は入っていますか。	sābisuryō wa haitte imasu
Could we have a/an . . . please?	…を下さい。	. . . o kudasai
ashtray	灰皿	haizara
bottle of . . .	…一本	. . . ippon
another chair	椅子をもう一つ	isu o mō hitotsu
chopsticks	箸	hashi
fork	フォーク	fōku
glass of water	水一杯	mizu ippai
knife	ナイフ	naifu
napkin	ナプキン	napukin
plate	皿	sara
spoon	スプーン	supūn
toothpick	爪楊	tsumayōji

FOR COMPLAINTS, see page 59

l like a/an/ ome . . .	…を下さい。	. . . o kudasai
eritif	アペリティフ	aperitīfu
ppetizer	オードーブル	ōdōburu
eer	ビール	bīru
ead	パン	pan
itter	バター	batā
ibbage	キャベツ	kyabetsu
ieese	チーズ	chīzu
iips (french fries)	フレンチフライドポテト	furenchi furaido poteto
offee	コーヒー	kōhī
essert	デザート	dezāto
sh	魚	sakana
uit	果物	kudamono
ame	猟鳥	ryōchō
e-cream	アイスクリーム	aisukurīmu
etchup	ケチャップ	kechappu
mon	レモン	remon
ttuce	レタス	retasu
eat	肉	niku
ilk	ミルク	miruku
ineral water	ミネラルウォーター	mineraru uōtā
ustard	からし	karashi
il	油	abura
epper	胡椒	koshō
otatoes	じゃがいも	jagaimo
ce	御飯	go-han
olls	ロールパン	rōru pan
alad	サラダ	sarada
alt	塩	shio
andwich	サンドウィッチ	sandoittchi
easoning	調味料	chōmiryō
iellfish	えび類	ebi rui
iack	スナック	sunakku
oup	スープ	sūpu
oaghetti	スパゲッティ	supagetti
tarter	オードーブル	ōdōburu
ugar	砂糖	satō
ea	紅茶	kōcha
egetables	野菜	yasai
inegar	酢	su
vater	水	mizu
rine	ぶどう酒	budōshu

What's on the menu?

Our menu reader is presented according to courses. Under ea heading you'll find an alphabetical list of dishes in Japanese wi their English equivalents. This serves two purposes. Firstly, i designed to help you make the most of both Japanese and We ern-style menus. It includes everyday terms and special dish Secondly, you can use the lists for personal shopping.

Here's our guide to good eating and drinking. Turn to the cou you want.

Obviously, you're not going to go through every course on t menu. If you've had enough, say:

Nothing more, thanks.	もう結構です。	mō kekkō desu

When ordering your meal, the best way to use our guide is show the waiter the food list (pp. 45 to 58). Let him point o on the list what's available at the moment.

FOR BREAKFAST, see page 35

ppetizers—Starters

like an appetizer.	オードブルをお願いします。	ōdōburu o o-negai shimasu
hat do you commend?	何かおいしい物がありますか。	nanika oishii mono ga arimasu ka

スパラガス	asuparagasu	asparagus tips
ンチョビー	anchobī	anchovies
勢えび	ise-ebi	lobster
わし	iwashi	sardines
ードーブル盛り合せ	ōdōburu moriawase	assorted appetizers
リーヴ	orību	olives
き	kaki	oysters
たつむり	katatsumuri	snails
に	kani	crabmeat
ャビア	kyabia	caviar
えび	kuruma-ebi	prawns
えび	ko-ebi	shrimp
の卵	sakana no tamago	roe
け	sake	salmon
ば	saba	mackerel
ラダ	sarada	salad
ラミ	sarami	salami
いか	suika	watermelon
ロリー	serori	celery
ーセージ	sōsēji	sausage
うがらし	tōgarashi	sweet (green) peppers
しん	nishin	herring
生の／くん製の	nama no/kunsei no	raw/smoked
まぐり	hamaguri	clams
ム	hamu	ham
ルーツジュース	furūtsu jūsu	fruit juice
ぐろ	maguro	tunny fish (tuna)
ッシュルーム	masshurūmu	mushrooms
ディシュ	radisshu	radishes

panese specialities

つまみ (otsumami) or きだし (tsukidashi) — These are both collective names for a Japanese-style appetizer. This may include many dishes, generally had with drinks. Ask the waiter to recommend one to you.

EATING OUT

Salad

Salad isn't an original part of the Japanese cuisine. Pickled veg tables are a more authentic equivalent. However, you can ord salads in Western-style restaurants.

What kinds of salad have you got?	どんなサラダがありますか。	don-na sarada ga arimasu ka

Soup

In the Japanese meal, soup is eaten simultaneously with (nev prior to) the main course (boiled rice and other items). In Wester style restaurants again, however, you can have Western-sty soups.

I'd like some soup.	スープをお願いします。	sūpu o o-negai shimasu.
What do you recommend?	何かおいしいスープがありますか。	nanika oishii sūpu ga arimasu ka

Egg dishes and omelets

There are no specific egg dishes or omelets in the authentic J panese cuisine, although eggs are very frequently used as i gredients. Omelet (called *omuretsu* in Japanese) is an impo from the West. You can have them in Western-style restauran

I'd like an omelet.	オムレツをお願いします。	omuretsu o o-negai shimas

卵豆腐 (tamagodōfu)	a kind of steamed-egg pudding in a square shape
卵焼 (tamagoyaki)	a Japanese-style omelet

Fish and seafood

I'd like some ... fish.	…をお願いします。	... o o-negai shimasu
What kinds of shellfish have you got?	どんなえびがありますか。	don-na ebi ga arimasu ka
あじ	aji	scad
まあじ	maaji	horse-mackerel
アンチョビ	anchobi	anchovy
伊勢えび	ise-ebi	lobster
いわし	iwashi	sardine
うなぎ	unagi	eel
かき	kaki	oyster
かに	kani	crab
かます	kamasu	pike
かわめんたい	kawamentai	burbot
かれい	karei	turbot/plaice
こい	koi	carp
小えび	ko-ebi	shrimp
車えび	kuruma-ebi	prawn
さけ	sake	salmon
さば	saba	mackerel
ざりがに	zarigani	crayfish
したびらめ	shitabirame	sole
しらうお	shirauo	whitebait
すずき	suzuki	perch
たら	tara	cod/haddock/whiting
にしん	nishin	herring
にしんのくん製	nishin no kunsei	kipper
はまぐり	hamaguri	clam
ひらめ	hirame	brill/halibut
ほうぼう	hōbō	gurnet
ほたて貝	hotategai	scallop
ぼら	bora	mullet
まぐろ	maguro	tunny (tuna)
ます	masu	trout

Seafood specialities

As a sea-surrounded island nation, Japan has developed, ove the centuries, a variety of seafood specialities unlike anything t be found in the rest of the world. Here are some of the most typica Japanese seafood dishes:

寿司
(sushi)

One of the most popular Japanese dishes, *sush* is worth giving a try. Here are some of th many varieties of *sushi:*

Nigiri-zushi consists of a slightly vinegary hand-pressed rice ball topped with slices c cooked egg and various seafoods (raw tunny swordfish, abalone, clam, octopus, squid shrimp, sea bream, sea bass, sole, tin mackerel, etc.).

Maki-zushi is recommended for first-timers It's a tiny roll of slightly vinegary rice wrap ped up in paperlike seaweed. Usually, there are fish and vegetables in the middle of th roll.

Sushi is usually eaten with the hands

刺身
(sashimi)

This is another Japanese seafood speciality which, though highly prized by the Japanese frightens foreigners off at the beginning *Sashimi* consists of little bitesized pieces o sliced fresh raw seafood (mostly tunny) and is served with soy sauce and green mustard (powerful Japanese radish mustard). Be care ful not to take too much of this special mustard which has no equivalent in the West! White rice accompanies *sashimi*. Usually *sake* i drunk to wash it down

天ぷら
(tempura)

Another well-known Japanese dish is *tempura* Fresh fish (horse-mackerel, cuttlefish, conger-eel, river trout, whitebait, etc.), shellfish (shrimp, clam, prawn, lobster, etc.) and fresh vegetables (spring carrots, kidney beans, onions, aubergines, parsley, garlic, pimiento, Japanese mushrooms, sliced lotus root, etc.) and potatoes are dipped in a batter of flour and egg and then quickly deep-fried in sesame or pure vegetable oil. You'll eat *tempura* preferably dipped in a special sauce (soy sauce flavoured with sweet *sake*). Add grated Japanese radish with Japanese pimiento powder or grated fresh ginger. White rice will also be served. You'll drink beer or *sake* or Japanese green tea with *tempura*.

For full appreciation of *tempura*, you should go to top *tempura* restaurants where the chef will cook it right in front of you.

Meat

What kinds of meat have you got?	どんな肉がありますか。	don-na niku ga arimasu ka
I'd like some . . .	…をお願いします。	. . . o o-negai shimasu
beef/pork/veal/ mutton	牛肉／豚肉／子牛肉／羊肉	gyūniku/butaniku/ koushiniku/yōniku

あばら肉	abaraniku	T-bone/rib steak
オックステール	okkusutēru	oxtail
カツレツ	katsuretsu	escalope
肩の肉	kata no niku	shoulder
肝臓	kanzō	liver
牛肉	gyūniku	beef
首	kubi	neck (best end)
鞍下肉	kurashitaniku	saddle
子牛	koushi	veal
子牛の脳味噌	koushi no nōmiso	calf's brains
子牛の膵臓	koushi no suizō	veal sweetbreads
子牛のロース肉	koushi no rōsuniku	veal cutlets
子羊	kohitsuji	lamb
子羊の骨付あばら肉	kohitsuji no honetsuki abaraniku	lamb chops
サーロイン	sāroin	sirloin
舌	shita	tongue
シチュー肉	shichū niku	stew
シャトーブリアン	chatōburian	chateaubriand
腎臓	jinzō	kidney
ステーキ	sutēki	steak
ソーセージ	sōsēji	sausage
トルヌドー	torunudo	tournedos
肉まんじゅう	nikumanju	rissoles
ハム	hamu	ham
冷肉盛り合せ	reiniku moriawase	cold cuts
ビフテキ	bifuteki	beef steak
豚肉	butaniku	pork
豚の骨付あばら肉	buta no honetsuki abaraniku	pork chops
ベーコン	bēkon	bacon
ヒレ肉	hireniku	fillet
骨付あばら肉	honetsuki abaraniku	chop
骨付あばら肉	honetsuki abaraniku	cutlet

トン	maton	mutton
の肉	mune no niku	breast
つ	motsu	tripe
も肉	momoniku	leg
ーストビーフ	rōsuto bīfu	roast beef
ーストポーク	rōsuto pōku	roast pork

low do you like your meat?

baked	天火焼した	tempiyaki shita
barbecued	バーベキューした	bābekyūshita
boiled	煮た	nita
braised	とろ火で煮た	torobi de nita
broiled	焦がした	kogashita
en casserole	土鍋で煮た	donabe de nita
fried	揚げた	ageta
grilled	焼いた	yaita
pot-roast	鍋焼きにした	nabeyaki ni shita
roast	ローストした	rōsutoshita
stewed	シチューにした	shichūnishita
stuffed	詰め物をした	tsumemono o shita
underdone (rare)	生焼き	nama yaki
medium	普通	futsū
well-done	良く焼く	yoku yaku

Japanese meat dishes

The Japanese weren't originally a meat-eating people. Part because of the Buddhist influence, meat was never part of th Japanese diet until introduced by Westerners about a centu ago. This explains why there's only a limited variety of Japane meat dishes.

We recommend you to have . . . ...がとてもおいしいです よ。 . . . ga totemo oishii desu

すきやき (sukiyaki)

This best-known Japanese meat dish consis of thin slices of tender beef, leeks, bean cu squares, thin noodles, burdock, all cooked an iron pan on the table in front of you. Th ingredients are simmered in an aromat mixture of soy sauce, *mirin* (sweet *sak* and water. The waitress will add spoonfuls sugar to the mixture.

You receive a small side bowl containing whipped raw egg into which you dip th *sukiyaki* morsels for cooling just before eatin Take whatever you choose from the cookir pan with your chopsticks.

You'll be served bowls of white rice to com plete the meal. You can drink either beer warm *sake* (rice wine) while eating *sukiyaki*

Game and fowl

'd like some game.	猟鳥をお願いします。	ryōchō o o-negai shimasu
What poultry dishes do you serve?	どんな鳥料理がありますか。	donna toriryori ga arimasu ka

ひる	ahiru	duck
ひるの子	ahiru no ko	duckling
のしし	inoshishi	wild boar
ずら	uzura	quail
ちょう	gacho	goose
じ	kiji	pheasant
豚	kobuta	suck(l)ing pig
ずめ	suzume	sparrow
わとり	niwatori	chicken
わとりの胸肉	niwatori no muneniku	chicken breast
ーストチキン	rosuto chikin	roast chicken
と	hato	pigeon
なばと	hinabato	squab
面鳥	shichimencho	turkey

き鳥 (yakitori)

Yakitori is skewered pieces of chicken, duck, quail and sparrow (whitemeat, gizzard, heart, kidney, leg, neck, sausage and skin) dipped in a special sweet soy sauce and then cooked over an open charcoal grill. Wash it down with *sake* or beer.

In a *yakitoriya* (restaurant specialized in *yakitori*), however, the meat used may well be pork or veal.

Vegetables and seasonings

What vegetables do you recommend?	何かいい野菜がありますか。	nani ka ii yasai ga arimasu ka
Are they fresh or canned?	新鮮な野菜ですか，それとも罐詰ですか。	shinsen na yasai desu ka soretomo kanzume desu ka
I'd prefer some salad.	私はサラダにします。	watashi wa sarada ni shimas

赤キャベツ	akakyabetsu	red cabbage
アスパラガス	asuparagasu	asparagus
いんげん豆	ingenmame	kidney beans
エジプト豆	ejiputomame	chick peas
えんどう豆	endōmame	peas
かぼちゃ	kabocha	marrow (zucchini)
カリフラワー	karifurawā	cauliflower
きくいも	kikuimo	Jerusalem artichokes
きくぢしゃ	kikujisha	endive
キャベツ	kyabetsu	cabbage
きゅうり	kyūri	cucumber
クレソン	kureson	watercress
小きゅうり	kokyūri	gherkins
米	kome	rice
莢いんげん	sayaingen	haricot (french) beans
サラダ	sarada	salad
西洋わさび	seiyōwasabi	horseradish
じゃがいも	jagaimo	potatoes
セロリ	serori	celery
そら豆	soramame	broad beans
玉ねぎ	tamanegi	onions
てんさい	tensai	beet(root)
とうもろこし	tōmorokoshi	corn on the cob
トマト	tomato	tomatoes
なす	nasu	aubergines (egg-plant)
にんじん	ninjin	carrots
にんにく	nin-niku	garlic
ねぎ	negi	leeks
パセリー	paseri	parsley
ピーマン	piiman	pimiento
マッシュルーム	masshurūmu	mushroom

キャベツ	mekyabetsu	brussels sprouts
ちとうもろこし	mochitōmorokoshi	sweet corn
菜盛り合せ	yasaimoriawase	mixed vegetables
ディシユ	adisshur	radishes
タス	retasu	lettuce
ンズ豆	renzumame	lentils

Vegetables may be served:

baked	天火焼した	tempiyaki shita
boiled	煮た	nita
chopped	切った	kitta
creamed	クリーム煮	kurīmu ni
diced	四角にきざんだ	shikaku ni kizanda
fried	揚げた	ageta
grilled	焼いた	yaita
roasted	ローストした	rōsuto shita
stewed	シチューした	shichū shita
stuffed	詰め物をした	tsumemono o shita

If you want vegetables to be served in a Western way, you should go to a Western-style or foreign restaurant.

Fruit

Do you have fresh fruit?	新鮮な果物がありますか。	shinsen na kudamono ga arimasu ka
I'd like a fresh fruit cocktail.	新鮮な果物のサラダをお願いします。	shinsen na kudamono no sarada o o-negai shimasu

アーモンド	āmondo	almonds
あんず	anzu	apricots
いちご	ichigo	strawberries
いちじく	ichijiku	figs
オリーブ	orību	olives
オレンジ	orenji	oranges
かき	kaki	persimmon
木いちご	kiichigo	raspberries
くり	kuri	chestnuts
くるみ	kurumi	walnuts
グレープフルーツ	gurēpu furūtsu	grapefruit
やしの実	yashi no mi	coconut
さくらんぼ	sakuranbo	cherries
すぐり	suguri	gooseberries
すいか	suika	watermelon
なし	nashi	pear
なつめやし	natsumeyashi	dates
パイナップル	painappuru	pineapple
はしばみの実	hashibami no mi	hazelnuts
バナナ	banana	banana
ぶどう	budō	grapes
プラム	puramu	plums
干しすもも	hoshi sumomo	prunes
みかん	mikan	tangerine
メロン	meron	melon
もも	momo	peach
りんご	ringo	apple
レモン	remon	lemon

essert

essert is foreign to the typical Japanese dishes. Called *dezāto* Japanese, it was introduced by Westerners about a century go. If you've survived all the courses on the menu, you may want say:

d like a dessert, lease.	デザートをお願いします。	dezāto o o-negai shimasu
omething light, lease.	何か軽い物をお願いします。	nanika karui mono o o-negai shimasu
ust a small portion.	ほんのわずかだけ。	hon-no wazuka dake
othing more, thanks.	これでもう結構です。	kore de mō kekko desu

f you're not sure what to order, ask the waiter:

Vhat do you have or dessert?	デザートは何がありますか。	dezāto wa nani ga arimasu ka
Vhat do you ecommend?	何がおいしいですか。	nani ga oishii desu ka

アモンドスフレ	āmondo sufure	almond soufflé
アイスクリーム	aisukurīmu	ice-cream
アイスクリームコーヒー	aisukurīmu kōhī	coffee ice-cream
アップルパイ	appurupai	apple pie
甘いオムレツ	amai omuretsu	sweet omelet
泡立てクリーム	awadate kurīmu	whipped cream
木いちごアイスクリーム	kiichigo aisukurīmu	raspberry ice-cream
木いちごスフレ	kiichigo sufure	frozen raspberry soufflé
ケーキ	kēki	cake
コーヒーケーキ	kōhī kēki	coffee cake
スフレ	sufure	soufflé
ストローベリーサンデー	sutoroberī sandē	strawberry sundae
チョコレートケーキ	chokorēto kēki	chocolate cake
チョコレートサンデー	chokorēto sandē	chocolate sundae
チョコレートプディング	chokorēto puddingu	chocolate pudding

なしの赤ぶどう酒煮	nashi no akabudōshu ni	pears baked in red wine
なしのクリーム煮	nashi no kurīmu ni	pears cooked with cream
パイナップルのキルシュ漬	painappuru no kirushu zuke	pineapple with kirsc (cherry brandy)
バナナ揚げ	banana age	banana fritters
バナナフランベ	banana furanbe	banana flambé
ピーチメルバ	pīchi meruba	peach Melba
プディング	pudingu	pudding
フルーツサラダ	furūtsu sarada	fruit cocktail
ラム入りオムレツ	ramu iri omuretsu	rum omelet
レモンアイスクリーム	remon aisukurīmu	lemon ice-cream
レモンスフレ	remon sufure	lemon soufflé

That's the end of our menu. For drinks, see page 60. But afte the feast comes. . .

The bill (check)

May I have the bill (check), please?	お勘定，お願いします。	okanjo, o-negai shimasu
Haven't you made a mistake?	間違いはありませんね。	machigai wa arimasen ne
Is service included?	サービス料は入っていますか。	sābisuryō wa haitte imasu k
Is the cover charge included?	テーブル代は入っていますか。	tēburudai wa haitte imasu k
Is everything included?	全部入っていますか。	zenbu haitte imasu ka
Do you accept traveller's cheques?	トラベラーチェックで払ってもいいですか。	toraberā chekku de haratte mo ii desu ka
Thank you, this is for you.	ありがとう，これはチップです。	arigatō. kore wa chippu desu
Keep the change.	おつりは入りません。	otsuri wa irimasen

サービス料込み
SERVICE INCLUDED

hat was a very good eal. We enjoyed it.	とてもいい食事でした。ごちそう様。	totemo ii shokuji deshita go-chisō sama
'e'll come again ome time.	又来ましよう。	mata kimashō

omplaints

ut perhaps you'll have something to complain about. . .

here's a draught ere. Could you give s another table?	ここは風があります。他のテーブルをお願いします。	koko wa kaze ga arimasu hoka no teburu o o-negai shimasu.
hat's not what I or-ered. I asked for . . .	これは注文と違います。…を注文しました。	kore wa chūmon to chigai-masu . . . o chūmon shimashita
don't like this/I an't eat this.	これは気に入りません／これはとても食べられません。	kore wa kiniirimasen/ kore wa totemo taberare masen
May I change this?	換えてもらえますか。	kaete moraemasu ka
'he meat is . . .	肉が…です	niku ga . . . desu
verdone/underdone	焼け過ぎ／生焼け	yakesugi/namayake
oo rare/too tough	殆ど生／固い	hotondo nama/katai
'his is too . . .	これは…過ぎです。	kore wa . . . sugidesu
itter/salty/sweet	苦／辛／甘	niga/kara/ama
'he food is cold.	これは冷たいですね。	kore wa tsumetai desu ne
'his is not fresh.	これは新鮮ではありません。	kore wa shinsen de wa arimasen
Would you ask the ead waiter to come over?	チーフにここに来るように言って下さい。	chīfu ni koko ni kuru yō ni itte kudasai

Drinks

Beer

There are several brands of popular Japanese-brewed beer *Asahi, Kirin, Sapporo* and *Suntory*. They're all pretty similar English and German lager beers.

If you're thirsty, say:

I'd like a (cold) beer, please.	(冷たい) ビールを下さい。	(tsumetai) bīru o kudasai

Sake

This heady Japanese national drink is distilled from rice an drunk generally warm (the right temperature is 98.6°F). It's drun from small porcelain cups.

If you would like to taste it, say:

May I have a cup of sake, please?	お酒を一杯お願いします。	o-sake o ippai o-negai shimasu

Wine

Wine isn't an authentic Japanese drink, and until recent Japanese wine didn't exist. There are now a few wine-producin vineyards in the centre of the country, but most wines served i restaurants are still imported from abroad. You'll find Italia wines in Italian restaurants, French wines in French restaurant etc. Don't expect to find wine in a *ryoriya* (Japanese-style re taurant).

I'd like . . . of . . .	…を…下さい。	. . . o . . . kudasai
a bottle	一本	ippon
half a bottle	半本	hanbon
a glass	一杯	ippai
a litre	一リットル	ichi rittoru

ᐯant a bottle of hite wine.	白ぶどう酒を一本下さい。	shirobudōshu o ippon kudasai
ow much is a bottle f . . . ?	…は一本いくらですか。	. . . wa ippon ikura desu ka
nat's too expensive.	高過ぎます。	takasugimasu
aven't you anything heaper?	何かもっと安いのはありませんか。	nanika motto yasui no wa arimasen ka
ne, that will do.	そう，それでいいです。	so, sorede īdesu

' you enjoyed the wine, you may want to say:

ring me another . . . ease.	もう…持って来て下さい。	mō . . . motte kite kudasai
'ass/bottle	一杯／一本	ippai/ippon
/hat's the name of is wine?	何と言うぶどう酒ですか。	nanto iu budōshu desu ka
/here does this wine ome from?	どこのぶどう酒ですか。	doko no budōshu desu ka
ow old is this wine?	何年の物ですか。	nannen no mono desu ka

dry	ドライ	dorai
red	赤い	akai
rosé	ローゼ	rōze
sparkling	泡の立つ	awanotatsu
sweet	甘い	amai
white	白い	shiroi
chilled	冷たくした	tsumetakushita
at room temperature	部屋の温度と同じ	heya no ondo to onaji

Other alcoholic drinks

Perhaps you would like to order one of the following drinks o one occasion or another:

aperitif	アペリティフ	aperitīfu
beer	ビール	bīru
brandy	ブランデー	burandē
cider	サイダー	saidā
cognac	コニャック	konnyakku
gin	ジン	jin
gin fizz	ジンフィズ	jin fīzu
gin and tonic	ジントニック	jin tonikku
liqueur	リキュール	rikyūru
port	ポートワイン	pōtowain
rum	ラム	ramu
sherry	シエリー	sherī
vermouth	ベルモット	berumotto
vodka	ウオッカ	uokka
screwdriver	スクリュードライバー	sukuryū doraibā
whisky	ウィスキー	uisukī
neat (straight) on the rocks	ストレート／オンザロック	sutorēto/onzarokku
whisky and soda	ハイボール	haibōru

glass	一杯	ippai
bottle	一本	ippon
single	シングル	shinguru
double	ダブル	daburu

Japan produces its own whisky, although Scotch is imported fron Scotland. One of the best Japanese brands is *Suntory*. Othe brands are *Nikka* and *Ocean*.

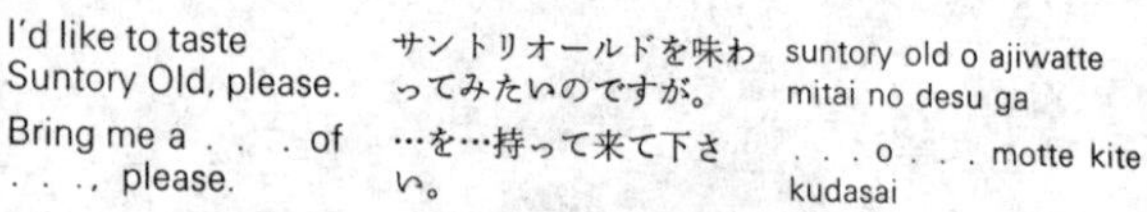

I'd like to taste Suntory Old, please.	サントリオールドを味わってみたいのですが。	suntory old o ajiwatte mitai no desu ga
Bring me a . . . of . . . ., please.	…を…持って来て下さい。	. . . o . . . motte kite kudasai

乾杯
(kanpai)
CHEERS!

Other beverages

I'd like a . . .	…を下さい。	. . . o kudasai
Have you any . . . ?	…がありますか。	. . . ga arimasu ka
chocolate	チョコレート	chokorēto
Coca-Cola	コカコーラ	koka kōra
coffee	コーヒー	kōhī
cup of coffee	コーヒー一杯	kōhī ippai
coffee with cream	クリーム入りコーヒー	kurīmu iri kōhī
espresso coffee	エクスプレッソコーヒー	ekkusupuresso kōhī
iced coffee	アイスコーヒー	aisu kōhī
fruit juice	フルーツジュース	furūtsu jūsu
grapefruit	グレープフルーツ	gurēpu jūsu
lemon/orange	レモン／オレンジ	remon/orenji
pineapple/tomato	パイナップル／トマト	painappuru/tomato
lemonade	レモナード	remonādo
fizzy/still	泡の立つ／泡の立たない	awa no tatsu/awa no tatanai
milk	ミルク	miruku
milk shake	ミルクセーキ	miruku sēki
mineral water	ミネラルウオーター	mineraru uōtā
orangeade	オランジエード	oranjiēdo
Pepsi-Cola	ペプシーコーラ	pepushi kōra
soda water	ソーダ水	sōdāsui
tea	紅茶	kōcha
with milk/lemon	ミルク入り／レモン	miruku iri/remon
tonic water	トーニックウオーター	tonikku uōtā

Eating light—Snacks

I'll have one of these, please.	これをひとつお願いします。	kore o hitotsu o-negai shimasu
Give me two of these and one of those.	これを二つとあれを一つ下さい。	kore o futatsu to are o hitots kudasai
to the left	左側の	hidarigawa no
to the right	右側の	migigawa no
above	上の	ue no
below	下の	shita no
Give me a/an/some . . . ., please.	…を下さい。	. . . o kudasai
beefburger	ビーフバーガー	bīfubāgā
biscuits (cookies)	ビスケット	bisuketto
bread	パン	pan
butter	バター	batā
cake	ケーキ	kēki
chocolate (bar)	(板) チョコレート	(ita) chokorēto
hamburger	ハンバーガー	hanbāgā
hot dog	ホットドッグ	hotto doggu
ice-cream	アイスクリーム	aisukurīmu
pastry	お菓子	o-kashi
pie	パイ	pai
roll	ロールパン	rōru pan
salad	サラダ	sarada
sandwich	サンドウィッチ	sandoitchi
sweets (candy)	キャンディ	kyandī
toast	トースト	tōsuto
waffles	ワッフル	waffuru
How much is it?	それはいくらですか。	sore wa ikura desu ka

EATING OUT

'ravelling around

'lane

'ery brief because at any airport you're sure to find someone who peaks English. But here are a few useful expressions you may 'ant to know. . .

)o you speak :nglish?	英語を話しますか。	eigo o hanashimasu ka
s there a flight to iapporo?	札幌行きの飛行機はありますか。	sapporo yuki no hikōki wa arimasu ka
Vhen's the next)lane to Sapporo?	次の札幌行きのフライトは何時ですか。	tsugi no sapporo yuki no furaito wa nanji desu ka
;an I make a con-nection to Fukuoka?	福岡に乗り継ぎ出来ますか。	fukuoka ni noritsugi dekimasu ka
'd like a ticket to Vew York.	ニューヨークまでの切符を欲しいのですが。	nyūyōku made no kippu o hoshii no desu ga
Vhat's the fare to 3angkok?	バンコックまでいくらですか。	bankokku made ikura desu ka
single (one-way)	片道	katamichi
return (roundtrip)	往復	ōfuku
Vhat time does the olane take off?	飛行機は何時に立ちますか。	hikōki wa nanji ni tachimasu ka
Vhat time do I have to check in?	何時にチェックインしなければなりませんか。	nanji ni chekkuin shinakereba narimasen ka
Vhat's the flight number?	フライト番号は何番ですか。	furaito bangō wa nanban desu ka
Vhat time do we arrive?	何時に着きますか。	nanji ni tsukimasu ka

到着 ARRIVAL	出発 DEPARTURE

Train

If you're worried about train tickets, times of departure etc., g to a *kōtsūkōsha* (Japan Travel Bureau) office where they spea English or ask at your hotel.

Train travel in Japan is fast and on time on the main lines. First class (green) coaches are comfortable with reclining seats. Fo boarding green-car coaches, you'll have to buy a green-ca ticket in addition to a regular ticket. Second-class coaches ar often crowded.

All station names and important signs are printed in English

Types of trains

The New Tokaido Line, called *shinkansen* in Japanese, is currently the world's fastest luxury railway service. Seat reservation is computer-controlled for both first and second class.

The line operates a super-express service between Tokyo and Okayama (4 hours, 20 min.), stopping at Nagoya, Kyoto, Osaka, Kobe and Himeji. A limited express service runs between Tokyo and Osaka, stopping at all intermediate stations (4 hours, 10 min.).

On the rest of the Japanese railway network, there are three major categories of trains:

特急 (tokkyū)	Long-distance express stopping only at main stations. Supplementary fare required.
急行 (kyūkō)	Normal long-distance train stopping at main stations. Supplementary fare required.
普通 (futsū)	Local train stopping at all stations.

To the railway station

Vhere's the railway tation?	駅はどこですか。	eki wa doko desu ka
'axi, please!	タクシーお願いします。	takushī o-negai shimasu
'ake me to the ailway station.	駅まで連れていって下さい。	eki made tsurete itte kudasai
Vhat's the fare?	いくらですか。	ikura desu ka

Tickets

Vhere's the . . . ?	…はどこですか。	. . . wa doko desu ka
nformation office	案内所	annaijo
eservations office	予約受付の窓口	yoyakuuketsuke no madoguchi
icket office	切符売場	kippuuriba
want a ticket to Osaka, second-class eturn (roundtrip).	大阪行き二等往復の切符を一枚お願いします。	ōsakayuki nitō-ōfuku no kippu o ichimai o-negai shimasu
'd like two singles to Nagoya.	名古屋までの片道二枚下さい。	nagoya made no katamichi nimai kudasai
How much is the fare o Kobe?	神戸までいくらですか。	kobe made ikura desu ka
s it half price for a child? He's thirteen.	子供は半額ですか。彼は13歳です。	kodomo wa hangaku desu ka. kare wa jūsan sai desu

Note: Children up to the age of 6 travel free. From 6 to 12 year olds pay half fare.

Possible answers

一等ですか二等ですか。	First or second class?
片道ですか往復ですか。	Single or return (one-way or roundtrip)?
半額は12歳までです。	**It's half price up to the age of 12.**
大人料金を頂かねばなりません。	**You'll have to pay full fare.**

FOR TAXI, see page 27

Further enquiries

Is it a through train?	これは直通列車ですか。	kore wa chokutsū-ressha desu ka
Does this train stop at Okayama?	この列車は岡山に止まりますか。	kono ressha wa okayama ni tomari masu ka
When is the . . . train to Osaka?	大阪行きの…列車は何時ですか。	ōsaka yuki no . . . ressha wa nanji desu ka
first/last/next	最初の／最後の／次の	saisho no/saigo no/tsugi no
What time does the train from Kyoto arrive?	京都からの列車は何時に着きますか。	kyōto kara no ressha wa nanji ni tsuki masu ka
What time does the train for Kobe leave?	神戸行きの列車は何時に出ますか。	kōbe yuki no ressha wa nanji ni demasu ka
Will the train leave on time?	予定通りに出ますか。	yotē dōri ni demasu ka
Is the train late?	遅れていますか。	okurete imasu ka
Is there a dining-car on the train?	食堂車が付いていますか。	shokudōsha ga tsuite imasu ka

入口	ENTRANCE
出口	EXIT
ホーム	TO THE PLATFORMS

Where's the . . . ?

Where's the . . . ?	…はどこですか。	. . . wa doko desu ka
bar	バー	bā
buffet	ビュフェ	byuffe
left luggage office	手荷物一時預かり所	tenimotsu-ichijiazukarijo
lost and found office	遺失物取扱所	ishitsubutsu-toriatsukaijo
newsstand	新聞売り場	shinbun-uriba
restaurant	食堂	shokudō
waiting room	待合室	machiaishitsu
Where are the toilets?	手洗はどこですか。	te-arai wa doko desu ka

latform (track)

hat track does the in for Osaka leave m?	大阪行きの列車は何番線から出ますか。	ōsaka yuki no ressha wa nanbansen kara demasu ka
hat track does the in from Osaka ive at?	大阪発の列車は何番線につきますか。	ōsaka hatsu no ressha wa nanbansen ni tsukimasu ka
here is platform 7?	7番線はどこですか。	nana-bansen wa doko desu ka
this the right atform for the train . . . ?	…行きの列車はここから出ますか。	. . . yuki no ressha wa koko kara demasu ka

Possible answers

これは直通列車です。	It's a direct train.
…で乗り換えて下さい。	You have to change at . . .
…で普通列車に乗り換えて下さい。	Change at . . . and get a local train.
…番線は…です。	Platform . . . is . . .
あそこです／下の階です	over there/downstairs
左側です／右側です	on the left/on the right
…行きの列車は…時…分に…番線から発車します。	The train to . . . will leave at . . . from platform . . .
…行きの……列車は…分遅れる見込みです。	The . . . train for . . . will be . . . minutes late.
…発の列車が…番線に到着いたします。	The train from . . . is now arriving at platform . . .
…分遅れる見込みです。	There'll be a delay of . . . minutes.

All aboard . . .

Excuse me. May I get past?	すみません。通ってもいいですか。	sumimasen. tōtte mo iidesu ka
Is this seat taken?	この席はふさがっていますか。	kono seki wa fusagatte ima[su] ka

禁煙
NO SMOKING

I think that's my seat.	そこは私の席ですが。	soko wa watashi no seki desu ga
What station is this?	ここはどこの駅ですか。	koko wa doko no eki desu k[a]
How long does the train stop here?	どの位停車しますか。	dono kurai teisha shimasu [ka]
Can you tell me at what time we get to Kyoto?	何時に京都に着くか教えて下さい。	nanji ni kyōto ni tsuku ka oshiete kudasai
When do we get to Kobe?	神戸にはいつ着きますか。	kōbe ni wa itsu tsukimasu [ka]

Some time on the journey the ticket-collector (*shashō*) will com[e] around and say: *Kippu o haiken sasete itadakimasu* (Tickets please).

Eating

You can get snacks and drinks in the buffet car and in the dining car when it isn't being used for main meals. On express trains waitresses come around with sweets, snacks and drinks. They also sell *ekiben* (station lunch) containing a typical Japanese lunch (boiled rice, fish cakes, cooked egg, fish, seasoned vegetables, etc.). This box lunch can also be bought at the stations during the train's stop.

leeping

re there any free ompartments in the eeping-car?	空いている寝台がありますか。	aite iru shindai ga arimasu ka
/here's the sleeping-ar?	寝台車はどこですか。	shindaisha wa doko desu ka
ompartments 18 nd 19, please.	寝台18番と19番はどこですか。	shindai jūhachi-ban to jūkyū-ban wa doko desu ka
/ould you make up ur berths?	寝台を用意して下さい。	shindai o yōi shite kudasai
/ould you call me at o'clock?	7時に起して下さい。	shichi-ji ni okoshite kudasai
/ould you bring me ome coffee in the norning?	朝 コーヒーを持って来て下さい。	asa kōhī o motte kite kudasai

aggage and porters

an you help me with ny bags?	私の荷物を運んで下さい。	watashi no nimotsu o hakonde kudasai
'ut them down here, lease.	ここに置いて下さい。	koko ni oite kudasai

.ost!

Ve hope you'll have no need for the following phrases during your rip. . . but just in case:

Vhere's the lost property office?	遺失物取扱所はどこですか。	ishitsubutsu-toriatsukaijo wa doko desu ka
've lost my . . .	…をなくしました。	. . . o nakushimashita
lost it in . . .	…でなくしました。	. . . de nakushimashita
t's very valuable.	非常に貴重なんです。	hijō ni kichō nan desu

:OR PORTERS, also see page 24

Timetables

If you intend to do a lot of train travel, it might be a good idea t buy a timetable. A condensed English-language timetable i available free of charge from the Japanese National Railway travel agencies or the tourist information office.

I'd like a timetable, please. 時刻表を下さい。 jikokuhyō o kudasai

Underground (subway)

The *chikatetsu* in Tokyo, Osaka, Nagoya and other big citie corresponds to the London underground or the New Yor subway. The lines extend from the centre to the outer suburbs A map showing the various lines and stations is displayed outsid every station. Pocket maps can be obtained at any station fror the ticket office or at newsstands and travel agencies.

Fares depend on distance. If you'd like to use the *chikatets* regularly, it would be advantageous to get a book of ticket *(kaisūken)*. This will mean a small saving on fares.

It may be better not to use the underground during rush hours for the trains can be extremely crowded.

Bus—Tram (streetcar)

In most cases you pay as you enter. In some cases you may find the driver also acting as the conductor. You can buy a book of tickets *(kaisūken)* for multiple journeys.

I'd like a book of tickets.	回数券を下さい。	kaisūken o kudasai
Where can I get a bus to . . . ?	…行きのバスの停留所はどこですか。	. . . yuki no basu no teiryūjo wa doko desu ka
What bus do I take for . . . ?	…行きのバスはどれですか。	. . . yuki no basu wa dore desu ka
Where's the . . . ?	…はどこですか。	. . . wa doko desu ka
bus stop	バスの停留所	basu no teiryūjo
terminal	終点	shūten
When is the . . . bus to . . . ?	…行きの…バスはいつですか。	. . . yuki no . . . basu wa itsu desu ka
first/last/next	最初の／最後の／次の	saisho no/saigo no/tsugi no
How often do the buses to . . . run?	…行きのバスは何分毎ですか。	. . . yuki no basu wa nanpun goto desu ka
How much is the fare to . . . ?	…までの料金はいくらですか。	. . . made no ryōkin wa ikura desu ka
Do I have to change buses?	バスを乗り換えなければいけませんか。	basu o norikae nakereba ikemasen ka
How long does the journey take?	どれ位掛かりますか。	dore kurai kakarimasu ka
Will you tell me when to get off?	いつ降りたら良いか教えて下さい。	itsu oritara yoi ka oshiete kudasai
I want to get off at . . .	…で降りたいのですが。	. . . de oritai no desu ga
Please let me off at the next stop.	次の停留所で降して下さい。	tsugi no teiryūjo de oroshite kudasai
May I have my luggage, please?	荷物を下さい。	nimotsu o kudasai

バス停留所	BUS STOP

Or try one of these to get around:

bicycle	自転車	jitensha
boat	ボート	bōto
motorboat	モーターボート	mōtābōto
rowboat	ローボート	rōbōto
sailboat	ヨット	yotto
helicopter	ヘリコプター	herikoputā
hitch-hiking	ヒッチハイク	hitchihaiku
horse-back riding	乗馬	jōba
hovercraft	ホーバークラフト	hobākurafuto
motorcycle	オートバイ	ōtobai

and if you're really stuck, just . . .

walk	歩く	aruku

Around and about—Sightseeing

ere we're more concerned with the cultural aspect of life than ith entertainment; and, for the moment, with towns rather than e countryside. If you want a guide book, ask. . .

an you recommend good guide book or. . . ?	…の為の良い案内書を教えて下さい。	. . . no tame no yoi annaisho o oshiete kudasai
s there a tourist ffice?	旅行案内所がありますか。	ryokō-annaisho ga arimasu ka
Vhere's the tourist formation centre?	観光案内所はどこですか。	kankō-annaisho wa doko desu ka
Vhat are the main oints of interest?	何が特に面白いですか。	nani ga toku ni omoshiroi desu ka
Ve're only here or . . .	ここには…しかいません。	koko ni wa . . . shika imasen
few hours	二三時間	ni-san-jikan
day	一日	ichi-nichi
hree days	三日間	mikka-kan
week	一週間	isshū-kan
an you recommend sightseeing tour?	遊覧コースを教えて下さい。	yūran kōsu o oshiete kudasai
Vhere does the bus tart from?	バスはどこから出ますか。	basu wa doko kara demasu ka
Vill it pick us up at he hotel?	ホテルに迎えに来ますか。	hoteru ni mukae ni kimasu ka
Vhat bus/tram o we want?	どのバス／電車に乗りますか。	dono basu/densha ni norimasu ka
ow much does the our cost?	そのコースはいくら掛かりますか。	sono kōsu wa ikura kakarimasu ka
Vhat time does the our start?	そのコースは何時に出ますか。	sono kōsu wa nanji ni demasu ka
Ve'd like to rent a car or the day.	車を一日借りたいのですが。	kuruma o ichi-nichi karitai no desu ga

OR TIME OF DAY, see page 178

Is there an English-speaking guide?	英語を話すガイドがいますか。	eigo o hanasu gaido ga imasu ka
Where's the/Where are the . . . ?	…はどこですか。	. . . wa doko desu ka
abbey	修道院	shūdōin
antique shop	骨董屋	kottōya
aquarium	水族館	suizokukan
art gallery	画廊	garō
botanical gardens	植物園	shokubutsuen
building	建物	tatemono
castle	城	shiro
cathedral	大聖堂	daiseidō
cave	岩屋	iwaya
cemetery	墓地	bochi
church	教会	kyōkai
concert hall	コンサートホール	konsāto hōru
convent	修道院	shūdōin
docks	ドック	dokku
downtown area	市内	shinai
exhibition	展覧会	tenrankai
factory	工場	kōjō
fortress	城砦	jōsai
fountain	泉	izumi
gardens	庭園	teien
glass-works	ガラス製品	garasusēhin
grotto	洞窟	dōkutsu
harbour	港	minato
lake	湖	mizuumi
law courts	裁判所	saibansho
library	図書館	toshokan
market	市場	ichiba
memorial	記念碑	kinenhi
monument	記念碑	kinenhi
mosque	回教寺院	kaikyōjiin
museum	博物館	hakubutsukan
observatory	天文台	tenmondai
opera house	オペラ座	operaza
palace (imperial)	宮殿	kyūden
park	公園	kōen
planetarium	プラネタリューム	puranetaryūmu
post office	郵便局	yūbinkyoku
shopping centre	ショピングセンター	shoppingu sentā

rine	神社	jinja
adium	競技場	kyōgijō
atue	像	zō
ock exchange	証券取引所	shoken-torihikijo
nagogue	ユダヤ教会	yudaya kyōkai
levision studios	テレビスタジオ	terebisutajio
mple	寺	tera
wer	塔	tō
wn centre	繁華街	hankagai
wn hall	市役所	shiyakusho
niversity	大学	daigaku
atermill	水車	suisha
o	動物園	dōbutsuen

dmission

the . . . open on undays? . . .	…は日曜日開いていますか。	. . . wa nichiyōbi aite imasu ka
hen does it open?	いつ開きますか。	itsu akimasu ka
hen does it close?	いつ閉りますか。	itsu shimarimasu ka
ow much is the dmission charge?	入場料はいくらですか。	nyūjōryō wa ikura desu ka
there any reduction r . . . ?	…の割引がありますか。	. . . no waribiki ga arimasu ka
udents/children	学生／子供	gakusē/kodomo
ave you a guide ook (in English)?	(英語の) 案内書がありますか。	(eigo no) annaisho ga arimasu ka
an I buy a atalogue?	カタログを下さい。	katarogu o kudasai
it all right to take ictures?	写真をとっても構いませんか。	shashin o tottemo kamai masen ka

入場無料	ADMISSION FREE
カメラ持込禁止	NO CAMERAS ALLOWED

Who—What—When?

What's that building?	あの建物は何ですか。	ano tatemono wa nan desu
Who was the . . .?	…は誰ですか。	. . . wa dare desu ka
architect	建築家	kenchikuka
artist	芸術家	geijutsuka
painter	画家	gaka
sculptor	彫刻家	chōkokuka
Who built it?	誰が建てたのですか。	dare ga tateta no desu ka
Who painted that picture?	誰が画いたのですか。	dare ga kaita no desu ka
When did he live?	いつの時代の人ですか。	itsu no jidai no hito desu k
When was it built?	いつ建てられましたか。	itsu tateraremashita ka
Where's the house where . . . lived?	…が住んでいた家はどこですか。	. . . ga sunde ita ie wa do desu ka
We're interested in . . .	…に興味を持っています。	. . . ni kyōmi o motte imas
antiques	骨董品	kottōhin
archaeology	考古学	kōkogaku
art	芸術	geijutsu
botany	植物学	shokubutsugaku
ceramics	陶磁器	tōjiki
coins	古銭	kosen
fine arts	美術	bijutsu
furniture	家具	kagu
geology	地質学	chishitsugaku
history	歴史	rekishi
medicine	医学	igaku
music	音楽	ongaku
natural history	博物学	hakubutsugaku
ornithology	鳥類学	chōruigaku
painting	絵画	kaiga
pottery	陶芸	tōgei
sculpture	彫刻	chōkoku
wild life	野生生物	yaseiseibutsu
zoology	動物学	dōbutsugaku
Where's the . . . department?	…部はどこですか。	. . . bu wa doko desu ka

ust the adjective you've been looking for . . .

s . . .	…ですね。	. . . desu ne
nazing	驚異	kyōi
vful	恐しい	osoroshī
autiful	美しい	utsukushī
oomy	陰気	inki
deous	気味が悪い	kimiga warui
teresting	面白い	omoshiroi
agnificent	立派	rippa
onumental	堂々たるもの	dōdōtarumono
erwhelming	圧倒的	attōteki
nister	不吉	fukitsu
range	奇妙	kimyō
upendous	巨大	kyodai
perb	見事	migoto
rrible	ひどい	hidoi
rrifying	恐ろしい	osoroshī
emendous	ものすごい	monosugoi
ly	醜い	minikui

hurch services

lthough Japan isn't a Christian nation basically, there are over million Christians in the country (about 1% of the total population), and you'll find churches in almost any Japanese city. hurch services are held on Sundays unless otherwise specified. ew are conducted in English, however.

there a . . . near ere?	…はこの近くにありますか。	. . . wa kono chikaku ni arimasu ka
rthodox church	ギリシャ正教教会	girishaseikyō kyōkai
otestant church	プロテスタント教会	purotesutanto kyōkai
atholic church	カトリック教会	katorikku kyōkai
nagogue	ユダヤ教会	yudaya kyōkai
osque	回教寺院	kaikyō jiin
t what time is high ass?	ミサは何時からですか。	misa wa nanji kara desu ka
/here can I find a iest who speaks nglish?	英語を話す神父さんはどこで見付けられるでしょうか。	eigo o hanasu shinpu san wa doko de mitsukerareru deshō ka

Relaxing

Cinema (movies)—Theatre

The cinema programme normally consists of one feature fil (occasionally two), a short documentary or a newsreel an advertisements. Often there's no intermission midway throug the feature. Showings start in the late morning and son continue through the night.

Theatre openings depend entirely on drama groups. You ca find out what's playing from newspapers and guide books. A major Western-style hotels you can easily find publications lik "Visitors' Guide". Foreign films aren't dubbed but run in the original version, sub-titled in Japanese.

Have you a copy of the "Visitors' Guide"?	外人旅行者用の案内書がありますか。	gaijin-ryokōsha-yō no annaisho ga arimasu ka
What's on at the cinema tonight?	今夜映画館で何をやっていますか。	konya eigakan de nani o yatte imasu ka
What's playing at the National Theatre?	国立劇場では何をやっていますか。	kokuritsugekijō de wa nani yatte imasu ka
What sort of play is it?	それはどんな劇ですか。	sore wa donna geki desu k
By whom is it?	原作者は誰ですか。	gensakusha wa dare desu k
Can you recommend (a) . . . ?	…を教えて下さい。	. . . o oshiete kudasai
good film	面白い映画	omoshiroi eiga
comedy	喜劇	kigeki
drama	戯曲	gikyoku
musical	ミュジカル	myūjikaru
revue	時事風刺劇	jijifushigeki
something light	何か軽いもの	nanika karuimono
thriller	スリラー	surirā
Western	西部劇	sēbugeki

: what theatre is at new play by . . . showing?	…の新しい劇はどこでやっていますか。	. . . no atarashii geki wa doko de yatte imasu ka
'here's that new film y . . . playing?	…の新しい映画はどこでやっていますか。	. . . no atarashii eiga wa doko de yatte imasu ka
'ho's in it?	どんな俳優が出ていますか。	donna haiyū ga dete imasu ka
'ho's playing the ad?	主演は誰ですか。	shuen wa dare desu ka
'ho's the director?	監督は誰ですか。	kantoku wa dare desu ka
'hat time does it egin?	何時に始まりますか。	nanji ni hajimarimasu ka
/hat time does the iow end?	何時に終わりますか。	nanji ni owarimasu ka
re there any tickets r tonight?	今晩の切符はまだありますか。	konban no kippu wa mada arimasu ka
want to reserve two ckets for the show n Friday evening.	金曜日の晩のショーを二枚予約したいのですが。	kinyōbi no ban no shō o ni-mai yoyaku shitai no desu ga
an I have a ticket for ie matinee on uesday?	火曜日のマチネを一枚お願いします。	kayōbi no matine o ichi-mai o-negai shimasu
want a seat in the talls (orchestra).	一階最前列の席をお願いします。	ikkai saizenretsu no seki o o-negai shimasu
ot too far forward/ ack.	余り前でなく／後。	amari mae de naku/ushiro
omewhere in the iddle.	真中あたり。	mannaka atari
ow much are the eats in the circle balcony)?	二階席はいくらですか。	nikai-seki wa ikura desu ka
lay I have a rogramme, please?	プログラムを下さい。	puroguramu o kudasai
an I check this oat?	コートを預けられますか。	kōto o azukeraremasu ka
lere's my ticket.	これが私の切符です。	kore ga watashi no kippu desu

A few words on the traditional Japanese theatre

There are three major forms of traditional theatre which a unique to Japan. They are *Noh, Kabuki* and *Bunraku.*

Noh, the oldest of Japanese stage arts dating back to the 13 century, is performed in slow motion by all male actors wea ing colourful, stiff 15th-century brocade costumes and wood masks. The stage has no scenery except a backdrop of painte pine trees and is open to the audience on three sides. *Noh* difficult for foreigners (and even for Japanese) to understand an appreciate.

Kabuki, originated in the 16th century, is just the opposite *Noh.* The stage is vast, costumes and settings gorgeous, the actio fast and continuous. All the players are men, and the fema characters are impersonated by actors who have been special trained to do it since early childhood. *Kabuki* plays can last fo as long as 10 hours, but you aren't required to sit through th whole performance.

Bunraku is a form of puppet drama unique to Japan and no always easy for foreigners to appreciate. Each doll, 3 to 4½ fe high, is manipulated by a master puppeteer and two black-cla assistants. The dolls move on a waist-high platform on stage.

Opera—Ballet—Concert

Where's the opera house?	オペラ座はどこですか。	opera za wa doko desu ka
Where's the concert hall?	コンサートホールはどこですか。	konsāto hōru wa doko desu ka
What's on at the opera tonight?	今晩はどんなオペラがありますか。	konban wa donna opera ga arimasu ka
Who's performing?	誰が出ますか。	dare ga demasu ka

/hat time does the rogramme start?	何時に上演開始ですか。	nanji ni jōen kaishi desu ka
Vhich orchestra is laying?	どのオーケストラがやっていますか。	dono ōkesutora ga yatte imasu ka
Vhat are they laying?	何をやっていますか。	nani o yatte imasu ka
Vho's the onductor?	指揮者は誰ですか。	shikisha wa dare desu ka

Possible answers

売切れました。	I'm sorry, we're sold out.
一階前方の座席は少ししかあいてません。	There are only a few seats in the circle (balcony) left.
切符を見せて頂けますか。	May I see your ticket?

Night clubs

Night clubs are pretty much the same the world over, particularly when it comes to inflated prices. You can expect to pay a cover charge. Your drinks will be expensive. The girls sitting around aren't there because they like the decor.

There are some reasonably-priced places that provide good entertainment, so ask around. But find out the prices before you order and allow for the various surcharges.

For most night clubs a dark suit is sufficient.

Can you recommend a good night club?	面白いナイトクラブを教えて下さい。	omoshiroi naito kurabu o oshiete kudasai
s there a floor show?	フロアショーがありますか。	furoa shō ga arimasu ka
What time does the floor show start?	フロアショーは何時に始まりますか。	furoa shō wa nanji ni hajimarimasu ka
s evening dress necessary?	夜会服を着る必要がありますか。	yakaifuku o kiru hitsuyō ga arimasu ka

And once inside . . .

A table for two, please.	二人用のテーブルをお願いします。	futari-yō no tēburu o o-negai shimasu
My name is . . . I've reserved a table for four.	私は…です。4人用のテーブルを予約してあります。	watashi wa . . . desu. yo-nin-yō no tēburu o yoyaku shite arimasu
We don't have a reservation.	予約していません。	yoyaku shite imasen

Note: The standard closing time for drinking places in Japan is 11 p.m., although a fair number of coffee shops and snack bars or restaurants stay open all night. If you like, you can also spend the night in a cinema in Tokyo: some show films all through the night during week-ends.

Geisha

Geisha are highly accomplished hostess-entertainers trained since their early childhood to sing, dance, play the *shamisen* (a Japanese string instrument) and pour *sake* (Japanese rice wine) for guests. Most of them start their career as *geisha* servants when they are quite young (at the age of seven or eight). The apprenticeship won't be over until they reach the age of twenty or so. *Geisha* are used by big Japanese businessmen to entertain and relax business guests. A *geisha's* main function is to break the ice among Japanese men. Most *geisha* never get married but end up becoming mistresses of wealthy clients. You can hire *geisha* to attend your party in a private room in a Japanese style restaurant, but the rate can be pretty high. There are about 60,000 registered *geisha* in Japan.

Dancing

Where can we go dancing?	どこでダンスが出来ますか。	doko de dansu ga dekimasu ka
Is there a dance hall anywhere here?	この辺にダンスホールがありますか。	konohen ni dansu hōru ga arimasu ka
There's a dance at the . . .	…でダンスがあります。	. . . de dansu ga arimasu
Would you like to dance?	踊りに行きましょうか。	odori ni ikimasho ka
May I have this dance?	踊って頂けませんか。	odotte itadakemasen ka

Do you happen to play . . . ?

On rainy days, this page may solve your problems.

Do you happen to play chess?	チェスをおやりになりますか。	chesu o oyari ni narimasu ka
I'm afraid I don't.	いいえやりません。	iie yarimasen
No. But I'll give you a game of draughts (checkers).	いいえ，でもチェッカーならやってもいいですよ。	iie demo chekkā nara yattemo ii desu yo
king	キング	kingu
queen	クィーン	kuīn
castle (rook)	ルック	rukku
bishop	ビショップ	bishoppu
knight	ナイト	naito
pawn	ポーン	pōn
Do you play cards?	トランプをやりますか。	toranpu o yarimasu ka
bridge	ブリッジ	burijji
whist	ホイスト	hoisuto
pontoon (blackjack)	ブラックチェッカー	burakku chekkā
poker	ポーカー	pōkā
ace	エース	ēsu
king	キング	kingu
queen	クィーン	kuīn
jack	ジャック	jakku
joker	ジョーカー	jōkā

Sport

In addition to the world-famous *jūdō* and *karate*, practically any sport played in the West is also popular in Japan (golf, tennis football [soccer], rugby, basketball, etc.). Baseball, introduced into Japan from the U.S. in the 19th century, is today as much Japanese as American, although it's still almost unknown in Europe. But Japan's real national sport, not to be missed during your stay, is *sumō* (fat-power wrestling). Seasonal 15-day tournaments are held alternatively in Tokyo, Nagoya, Osaka and Fukuoka. Most *sumō* wrestlers are Japanese mastodons weighing from 230 to 350 pounds.

Where's the nearest golf course?	最寄りのゴルフ場はどこですか。	moyori no gorufujō wa doko desu ka
Where are the tennis courts?	テニスコートはどこですか。	tenisu kōto wa doko desu ka
Can I/we hire . . . ?	…を借りられますか。	. . . o kariraremasu ka
clubs	クラブ	kurabu
equipment	道具	dōgu
rackets	ラケット	rakketo
What's the charge per hour/day/round?	1時間／1日／1ラウンドの料金はいくらですか。	ichi-jikan/ichi-nichi/ichi-raundo no ryōkin wa ikura desu ka
What's the admission charge?	入場料はいくらですか。	nyūjōryō wa ikura desu ka
Is there a swimming pool here?	ここにプールがありますか。	koko ni pūru ga arimasu ka
Is it open-air or indoor?	屋外プールですか　屋内プールですか。	okugaipūru desu ka　okunai pūru desu ka
Is it heated?	暖房してありますか。	danbō shite arimasu ka
Is there any good fishing around here?	いい釣場がこの近くにありますか。	ii tsuriba ga kono chikaku ni arimasu ka
Is there any sumo match this evening?	今日相撲がありますか。	kyō sumō ga arimasu ka

On the beach

What's the beach ike?	どんな海水浴場ですか。	donna kaisuiyokujō desu ka
sandy/shingle/rocky	砂浜／砂利／岩場	sunahama/jari/iwaba
s it safe for swimming?	泳いでも大丈夫ですか。	oyoide mo daijōbu desu ka
s there a lifeguard?	見張人がいますか。	miharinin ga imasu ka
s it safe for children?	子供が泳いでも大丈夫ですか。	kodomo ga oyoidemo daijōbu desu ka
t's very calm.	とても穏やかです。	totemo odayaka desu
There are some big waves.	大波があります。	ōnami ga arimasu
Are there any dangerous currents?	流れの危険な所がありますか。	nagare no kiken-na tokoro ga arimasu ka
What time is high ide?	満潮はいつですか。	manchō wa itsu desu ka
What time is low ide?	干潮はいつですか。	kanchō wa itsu desu ka
What's the emperature of the water?	水温はいくらですか。	suion wa ikura desu ka
want to hire . . .	…を借りたいのですが。	. . . o karitai no desu ga
an air mattress	エアマットレス	eyā matto resu
a bathing hut	脱衣室	datsuishitsu
a deck chair	デッキチェアー	dekki chea
skin-diving equipment	スキンダイビング用道具	sukin daibingu yō dogu
a sunshade	日よけ	hiyoke
a surf board	サーフィン用板	sāfin yō ita
a tent	テント	tento
some water skis	水上スキー	suijōsukī
Where can I ent . . . ?	どこで…を借りられますか。	doko de . . . o karirare masu ka
a canoe	カヌー	kanū
a rowboat	ボート	bōto
a motor boat	モーターボート	mōtābōto
a sailboat	ヨット	yotto

What's the charge per hour?	一時間の料金はいくらですか。	ichi-jikan no ryōkin wa ikura desu ka

私有地
PRIVATE BEACH

遊泳禁止
NO BATHING

Obviously, not the place for us. Let's move on.

Winter sports

I'd like to go to a skating rink.	スケート場に行きたいのですが。	sukētojō ni ikitai no desu ga
Is there one near here?	この辺にありますか。	kono hen ni arimasu ka
I want to rent some skates.	スケートを借りたいのですが。	sukēto o karitai no desu ga
What are the skiing conditions like at. . . ?	…でのスキー条件はどうですか。	. . . de no sukī-jōken wa dōdesu ka
The snow is a little soft.	雪の質はちょっと柔らかです。	yuki no shitsu wa chotto yawaraka desu
Can I take skiing lessons there?	そこでスキーのレッスンが受けられますか。	soko de sukī no ressun ga ukeraremasu ka
Is there a ski lift?	スキーリフトがありますか。	sukīrifuto ga arimasu ka
I want to rent some skiing equipment.	スキー用具を借りたいのですが。	sukī yōgu o karitai no desu ga

;ountryside—Camping

 you wish to explore the Japanese countryside, here are a few ırases and a list of words that may be useful to you.

ɔw far is it to . . . ?	…までどの位ですか。	. . . made dono kurai desu ka
ɔw far is the next llage?	次の村までどの位ですか。	tsugino mura made dono kurai desu ka
'e we on the right ad to . . . ?	これは…に行く正しい道ですか。	kore wa . . . ni iku tadashii michi desu ka
'here does this road ad to?	この道はどこに行く道ですか。	kono micih wa doko ni iku michi desu ka
ɑn you show us ı the map where e are?	この地図で私達がどこに居るか教えて下さい。	kono chizu de watashitachi ga doko ni iru ka oshiete kudasai

andmarks

ırn	納屋	naya
idge	橋	hashi
ook	小川	ogawa
ıilding	建物	tatemono
ınal	運河	unga
ıurch	教会	kyōkai
ıff	崖	gake
ɔpse	柴	shiba
ɔrnfield	麦畑	mugi batake
ɔttage	小屋	koya
ırm	農家	nōka
ırry	渡し舟	watashibune
eld	野原	nohara
ɔotpath	遊歩道	yuhodō
ɔrest	森林	shinrin
amlet	小村	shōson
eath	灌木	kanboku
ill	丘	oka
ɔuse	家	ie

inn	宿屋	yadoya
lake	湖	mizuumi
marsh	沼地	numachi
moorland	荒野	kōya
mountain	山	yama
mountain range	山脈	sanmyaku
path	径	komichi
peak	峰	mine
plantation	農園	nōen
pond	池	ike
pool	プール	pūru
river	川	kawa
road	道	michi
spring	泉	izumi
stream	小川	ogawa
swamp	湿地	shitchi
track	小道	komichi
tree	木	ki
valley	谷	tani
village	村	mura
vineyard	ぶどう園	budōen
water	水	mizu
waterfall	滝	taki
well	井戸	ido
wood	森	mori
What's the name of the river?	この川の名前は何と言いますか。	kono kawa no namae wa nanto iimasu ka
How high is that mountain?	あの山はどの位の高さですか。	ano yama wa dono kurai n takasa desu ka
How high are those hills?	あの丘はどの位の高さですか。	ano oka wa dono kurai n takasa desu ka
Is there a scenic route to . . . ?	…に行く景色の良い道がありますか。	. . . ni yuku keshiki no y michi ga arimasu ka

. . .and if you're tired of walking, you can always try hitch hiking, though you may have to wait a long time for a lift.

Can you give me a lift to . . . ?	…まで乗せて下さい。	. . . made nosete kudasa

CAMPING

'amping

here are a fair number of camping sites in Japan. You can also ımp on private land, but get permission from the owner first.

an we camp here?	ここでキャンプしてもいいでしょうか。	koko de kyanpu shite mo ii deshō ka
this an official amping site?	ここは公認のキャンプ場ですか。	koko wa kōnin no kyanpujō desu ka
there drinking 'ater?	飲料水がありますか。	inryōsui ga arimasu ka
re there . . . ?	…がありますか。	ga arimasu ka
aths	風呂	furo
ıowers	シャワー	shawā
›ilets	手洗	te-arai
ıopping facilities	売店	baiten
there a youth ostel anywhere ear here?	この辺にユースホステルがありますか。	konohen ni yūsu hosuteru ga arimasu ka
o you know ıyone who can put s up for the night?	一晩だけ私達を泊めてくれそうな人を知りませんか。	hitoban dake watashitachi o tomete kuresō na hito o shirimasen ka

'he government-sponsored *Kokumin Shukusha* (public lodges) ı the countryside, although primarily designed for natives, wel- ɔme foreign tourists as well. There are currently about 350 ıch lodges in Japan, and both Japanese- and Western-style rooms re available. Meals are served in a communal dining room.

'ou may also like to try one of the twenty-odd *Kokumin Kyūka Aura* (public vacation villages) located in national park areas. acilities include camping sites. Meals are served in a communal ining room.

Making friends

Introduction

Here are a few phrases to get you started.

How are you?	お元気ですか。	ogenki desu ka
Very well, thank you.	元気です。お陰様で。	genki desu. o-kage sama d
How's it going?	いかがですか。	ikaga desu ka
Fine, thanks. And you?	元気です。お陰様で。貴方は。	genki desu. o-kage sama d anata wa
May I introduce Miss Philips?	フィリップスさんをご紹介します。	firippusu san o go-shōkai shimasu
I'd like you to meet a friend of mine.	私の友人をご紹介したいのですが。	watashi no yūjin o go-shōk shitai no desu ga
John, this is . . .	ジョン，こちらは…さんです。	jon. kochira wa . . san des
My name's . . .	私は…と申します。	watashi wa . . . to mōshi masu
Nice to meet you.	始めましてどうぞよろしく。	hajimemashite. dōzo yoroshiku

Follow-up

How long have you been here?	ここにもうどの位いらっしゃいますか。	koko ni mō dono kurai irasshaimasu ka
We've been here a week.	もう一週間になります。	mō isshū-kan ni narimasu
Is this your first visit?	ここには始めていらっしゃったのですか。	koko ni wa hajimete irassha no desu ka
No, we came here last year.	いいえ，昨年来ました。	iie sakunen kimashita
Are you enjoying your stay?	ここがお気に入りましたか。	koko ga o-kiniirimashita ka

es, I like . . . very uch.	はい…は非常に好きです。	hai . . . wa hijō ni suki desu
re you on your wn?	おひとりですか。	o-hitori desu ka
m with . . .	…と一緒です。	. . . to issho desu
y wife	家内	kanai
y family	家族	kazoku
y parents	両親	ryōshin
ome friends	友達	tomodachi
Vhere do you come om?	どこの国からこられましたか。	doko no kuni kara korare mashita ka
Vhat part of . . . o you come from?	…のどの辺からこられましたか°	. . . no donohen kara kora remashita ka
m from . . .	私は…からです。	watashi wa . . . kara desu
o you live here?	ここにお住いですか。	koko ni o-sumai desu ka
m a student.	私は学生です。	watashi wa gakusei desu
Vhat are you tudying?	何を勉強していますか。	nani o benkyo shite imasu ka
Ve're here on oliday.	休暇で来ています。	kyūka de kite imasu
m here on a usiness trip.	仕事で来ています。	shigoto de kite imasu
Vhat kind of usiness are you in?	お仕事は何ですか。	o-shigoto wa nan desu ka
hope we'll see you gain soon.	又お目に掛かれるといいですね。	mata o-me ni kakareruto ii desu ne
ee you later/See ou tomorrow.	では又後程／では又明日。	dewa mata nochi hodo/dewa mata ashita
m sure we'll run nto each other gain sometime.	又いつかお会い出来るでしょう。	mata itsuka o-ai dekiru deshō

The weather

They talk about the weather just as much in Japan as the Britis are supposed to do. So. . .

What a lovely day!	いいお天気ですね。	ii o-tenki desu ne
What awful weather.	何と悪い天気でしょう。	nanto warui tenki deshō
Isn't it cold today?	今日は寒いですね。	kyō wa samui desu ne
Isn t it hot today?	今日は暑いですね。	kyō wa atsui desu ne
Is it usually as warm as this?	いつもこんなに暖かいですか。	itsumo konna ni atatakai desu ka
It's very foggy, isn't it?	ひどい霧ですね。	hidoi kiri desu ne
What's the temperature outside?	外の気温はどの位ですか。	soto no kion wa dono kurai desu ka
The wind is very strong.	非常に強い風が吹いてます。	hijō ni tsuyoi kaze ga fuite imasu

Invitations

My wife and I would like you to dine with us on. . .	…に家内と共に貴方を夕食にお招きしたいのですが。	. . . ni kanai to tomo ni anata o yūshoku ni o-manek shitai no desu ga
Can you come to dinner tomorrow night?	明晩晩餐においで頂けますか。	myōban bansan ni o-ide itadakemasu ka
We're giving a small party tomorrow night. I do hope you can come.	明晩ささやかなパーティをしょうと思っています。貴方に来て頂けるとうれしいのですが。	myōban sasayaka na pātī o shiyō to omotte imasu. anata ni kite itadakeru to ureshii no desu ga
Can you come round for cocktails this evening?	今晩カクテルパーティにおいで頂けますか。	konban kakuteru pātī ni o-id itadakemasu ka
There's a party. Are you coming?	パーティがあります。いらっしゃいますか。	pātī ga arimasu. irasshai masu ka

That's very kind of you.	どうもありがとうございます。	dōmo arigatō gozaimasu
Great. I'd love to come.	すばらしい。喜んで寄せて頂きます。	subarashii. yorokonde yosete itadakimasu
What time shall we come?	何時にお伺いすればいいでしょうか。	nanji ni o-ukagai sureba ii deshō ka
May I bring a friend?	友達を一人連れて行ってもいいですか。	tomodachi o hitori tsurete itte mo ii desu ka
I'm afraid we've got to go now.	もうそろそろおいとましなければなりません。	mō sorosoro oitoma shinakereba narimasen
Next time you must come and visit us.	この次は私達の所においで下さい。	kono tsugi wa watashitachi no tokoro ni o-ide kudasai
Thank you very much for an enjoyable evening.	とても楽しい夕べを過ごさせて頂きどうもありがとうございました。	totemo tanoshii yūbe o sugosasete itadaki dōmo arigatō gozaimashita
Thanks for the party. It was great.	どうもありがとう。とてもすてきでした。	dōmo arigatō. totemo suteki deshita

Dating

Would you like a cigarette?	たばこはいかがですか。	tabako wa ikaga desu ka
Have you got a light, please?	火を貸して頂けますか。	hi o kashite itadakemasu ka
Can I get you a drink?	お飲み物を差し上げましょうか。	o-nomimono o sashiage mashō ka
Excuse me, could you help me, please?	恐れ入りますが。	osoreirimasu ga
I'm lost. Can you show me the way to . . . ?	道に迷いました。…へ行く道を教えて下さい。	michi ni mayoimashita. . . . e yuku michi o oshiete kudasai
You've dropped your handkerchief.	ハンカチを落としましたよ。	hankachi o otoshimashita yo
Are you waiting for someone?	誰かをお待ちですか。	dareka o o-machi desu ka

Are you free this evening?	今晩お暇ですか。	konban o-hima desu ka
Would you like to go out with me tonight?	今晩私と一緒に出掛けませんか。	konban watashi to issho ni dekakemasen ka
Would you like to go dancing?	ダンスをしに行きませんか。	dansu o shi ni ikimasen ka
I know a good dance hall.	良いダンスホールを知っています。	yoi dansu hōru o shitte imasu
Shall we go to the cinema (movies)?	映画でも見に行きましょうか。	eiga demo mi ni ikimashō ka
Would you like to go for a drive?	ドライブに行きましょうか。	doraibu ni ikimashō ka
I'd love to, thank you.	ええ。喜んで。	ee yorokonde
Where shall we meet?	どこで落ち合いましょうか。	doko de ochiaimashō ka
I'll pick you up at your hotel.	ホテルにお迎えに来ます。	hoteru ni o-mukae ni kimasu
I'll call for you at 8.	8時にお迎えに来ます。	hachi-ji ni o-mukaeni kimasu
May I take you home?	お宅までお送りしましょうか。	o-taku made ōkuri shimashō ka
Can I see you again tomorrow?	明日又お会い出来ますか。	asu mata o-ai dekimasu ka
Thank you, it's been a wonderful evening.	ありがとう。楽しい晩でした。	arigato. tanoshii ban deshita
What's your telephone number?	貴方の電話番号は。	anata no denwabango wa
Do you live alone?	おひとりですか。	o-hitori desu ka

Shopping guide

This shopping guide is designed to help you find what you want with ease, accuracy and speed. It features:

1. a list of all major shops, stores and services;
2. some general expressions required when shopping to allow you to be specific and selective;
3. full details of the shops and services most likely to concern you. Here you will find advice, alphabetical lists of items and conversion charts listed under the headings below.

Shops, stores and services

If you have a pretty clear idea of what you want before you se out, do a little homework first. Look under the appropriate head ing, pick out the article and find a suitable description for i (colour, material, etc.).

Shops in Japan usually open at around 9–10 a.m. and stay ope generally up to 9 p.m. except department stores which close a 5.30 or 6 p.m. All shops close one day per week; many are ope on Saturdays and Sundays. If you urgently need something, g to a major railway station where you can find a big shoppin centre open until almost 9 p.m.

Some stores in the larger towns offer a discount for traveller' checks or arrange sales tax rebates.

Where's the nearest . . . ?	最寄りの…はどこですか。	moyori no . . . wa doko desu ka
antique shop	骨董屋	kottōya
art gallery	画廊	garō
baker's	パン屋	panya
bank	銀行	ginkō
barber's	床屋	tokoya
beauty parlour	美容院	biyōin
bookshop	本屋	honya
bookstall	本を売っている店	hon o utte iru mise
butcher's	肉屋	nikuya
cable office	電報局	denpōkyoku
camera store	カメラ屋	kameraya
candy store	菓子屋	kashiya
chemist's	薬屋	kusuriya
cigar store	タバコ屋	tabakoya
confectionery	菓子屋	kashiya
dairy	牛乳屋	gyūnyūya
delicatessen	食料品店	shokuryōhinten
dentist	歯医者	haisha
department store	デパート	depāto
doctor	医者	isha
draper's (dry goods store)	生地屋	kijiya
dressmaker's	洋服屋	yōfukuya

drugstore	薬屋	kusuriya
dry cleaner's	クリーニング屋	kurininguya
filling station	ガソリンスタンド	gasorin-sutando
fish monger	魚屋	sakanaya
florist's	花屋	hanaya
furrier's	毛皮屋	kegawaya
garage	ガレージ	garēji
greengrocer's	八百屋	yaoya
grocery	食料品店	shokuryōhinten
hairdresser's (ladies)	美容院	biyōin
hardware store	金物屋	kanamonoya
hat shop	帽子屋	bōshiya
hospital	病院	byōin
jeweller's	宝石店	hōsekiten
launderette	貸し洗濯機屋	kashisentakukiya
laundry	洗濯屋	sentakuya
liquor store	酒屋	sakaya
market	市場	ichiba
milliner's	婦人帽子店	fujinbōshiten
news agent's	新聞店	shinbunten
newsstand	新聞売店	shinbunbaiten
optician	眼鏡屋	meganeya
pastry shop	菓子屋	kashiya
pawnbroker	質屋	shichiya
pharmacy	薬屋	kusuriya
photographer	写真師	shashinshi
photo store	写真屋	shashinya
police station	交番	kōban
post office	郵便局	yūbinkyoku
shirt maker's	ワイシャツ屋	waishatsuya
shoemaker's (repairs)	靴屋	kutsuya
shoe shop	靴屋	kutsuya
souvenir shop	みやげ物屋	miyagemonoya
sporting goods shop	スポーツ用品店	supōtsu yōhinten
stationer's	文房具店	bunbōguten
supermarket	スーパーマーケット	sūpāmāketto
tailor's	洋服屋	yōfukuya
tobacconist's	たばこ屋	tabakoya
toy shop	おもちゃ屋	omochaya
travel agent	旅行代理店	ryokō-dairiten
veterinarian	獣医	jūi
watch maker's	時計屋	tokēya
wine merchant's	酒屋	sakaya

General expressions

Here are some expressions which will be useful to you when you'r out shopping.

Where?

Where's a good . . . ?	良い…はどこですか。	yoi . . . wa doko desu ka
Where can I find a . . . ?	…はどこにありますか。	. . . wa doko ni arimasu ka
Where do they sell . . . ?	…はどこで売ってますか。	. . . wa doko de uttemasu ka
Can you recommend an inexpensive . . . ?	安い…を教えて下さい。	yasui . . . o oshiete kudasai
Where's the main shopping centre?	ショッピングセンターはどの辺にありますか。	shoppingu sentā wa donohen ni arimasu ka
How far is it from here?	ここからどの位の距離がありますか。	koko kara dono kurai no kyori ga arimasu ka
How do I get there?	そこにはどう行ったらいいですか。	soko ni wa dō ittara ii desu ka

Service

Can you help me?	お願いします。	o-negai shimasu
I'm just looking around.	見せてもらっている所です。	misete moratte iru tokoro desu
I want . . .	…が欲しいのですが。	. . . ga hoshii no desu ga
Can you show me some . . . ?	…を見せて下さい。	. . . o misete kudasai
Have you any . . . ?	…がありますか。	. . . ga arimasu ka

That one

Can you show me . . . ?	…を見せて下さい。	. . . o misete kudasai
that/those	あれ	are
the one in the window	ショーウインドーに出ているもの	shō uindō ni deteiru mono
It's over there.	あそこにあります。	asoko ni arimasu

Preference

prefer something of etter quality.	もっと質の良いのが欲しいのですが。	motto shitsu no yoi no ga hoshiino desu ga
Can you show me ome more?	もっと他のを見せて下さい。	motto hoka no o misete kudasai
Haven't you nything . . . ?	何か…のはありませんか。	nanika . . . no wa arimasen ka
heaper/better arger/smaller	もっと安い／もっと良い もっと大きな／もっと小さな	motto yasui/motto yoi motto ōki na/motto chiisa na

Defining the article

'd like a . . .	…を下さい。	. . . o kudasai
want a . . . one.	…のが欲しいのですが。	. . . no ga hoshiino desu ga
big	大きい	ōkii
cheap	安い	yasui
dark	色の濃い	iro no koi
good	良い	yoi
heavy	重い	omoi
arge	大きい	ōkii
ight (weight)	軽い	karui
ight (colour)	色の薄い	iro no usui
ectangular	長方形	chōhōkē
ound	丸い	marui
small	小さい	chīsai
square	四角い	shikakui
don't want anything oo expensive.	余り高いのは入りません。	amari takai no wa irimasen

How much?

How much is this?	これはいくらですか。	kore wa ikura desu ka
don't understand. Please write it down.	分かりません。 書いて下さい。	wakarimasen. kaite kudasai
don't want to spend more than 10,000 yen.	10,000円以上は使いたくないのですが。	ichiman yen ijō wa tsukaitaku nai no desu ga

FOR COLOURS, see page 111

Decision

That's just what I want.	私が欲しいのとピッタリ合います。	watashi ga hoshiino to pitta[illegible] aimasu
No, I don't like it.	これは好みに合いません。	kore wa konomi ni aimasen
I'll take it.	これにします。	kore ni shimasu

Ordering

Can you order it for me?	それを注文して頂けますか。	sore o chūmon shite itadake masu ka
How long will it take?	どの位掛かりますか。	dono kurai kakarimasu ka

Delivery

I'll take it with me.	持って帰ります。	motte kaerimasu
Deliver it at the . . . Hotel.	…ホテルに届けて下さい。	. . . hoteru ni todokete kudasai
Please send it to this address.	この住所に送って下さい。	kono jūsho ni okutte kudas[illegible]
Will I have any difficulty with the customs?	税関で問題になるような事はないでしょうね。	zeikan de mondai ni naru y[illegible] na koto wa nai deshō ne

Paying

How much is it?	いくらですか。	ikura desu ka
Can I pay by traveller's cheque?	トラベラーチェックで払えますか。	toraberā chekku de haraemasu ka
Do you accept credit cards?	クレジットカードでもよろしいですか。	kurejitto kādo demo yoroshi[illegible] desu ka
Haven't you made a mistake in the bill?	勘定に間違いはありませんか。	kanjō ni machigai wa arimasen ka
Can I have a receipt, please?	領収書を下さい。	ryōshūsho o kudasai
Will you wrap it, please?	包んで下さい。	tsutsunde kudasai
Do you have a carrier bag?	紙袋がありますか。	kamibukuro ga arimasu ka

nything else?

o, thanks, that's all.	これで結構です。	kore de kekkō desu
es, I want . . . / how me . . .	…が欲しいのですが／…を見せて下さい。	. . . ga hoshii no desu ga/ . . . o misete kudasai
hank you. Good-ye.	ありがとう。さようなら。	arigatō. sayonara

issatisfied

an you exchange nis, please?	これを交換して下さい。	kore o kōkan shite kudasai
want to return this.	これをお返しします。	kore o o-kaeshi shimasu
d like a refund. lere's the receipt.	お金を返して頂きたいのです。これが領収書です。	okane o kaeshite itadakitai no desu. kore ga ryōshūsho desu

Possible answers

いらっしゃいませ。	Can I help you?
何をお求めでいらっしゃいますか。	What would you like?
…をお求めでいらっしゃいますか。	What . . . would you like?
どういう色／どういう形 どんな質／どの位	colour/shape quality/quantity
あいにく全然ございません。	I'm sorry, we haven't any.
注文いたしましようか。	Shall we order it for you?
お持ち帰りになりますか。それともお届けしましょうか。	Will you take it with you or shall we send it?
これは…円です。	That's . . . yen, please.
…はお断わりしております。	We don't accept . . .
クレジットカード トラベラーチェック 銀行小切手	credit cards traveller's cheques personal cheques

Bookshop—Stationer's—News stand

In Japan, bookshops and stationer's are usually separate shop Newspapers and magazines are sold at kiosks.

Where's the nearest . . . ?	最寄りの…はどこですか。	moyori no . . . wa doko desu ka
bookshop	本屋	honya
stationer's	文房具店	bunbōguten
newsstand	新聞売店	shinbunbaiten
Where can I buy an English-language newspaper?	英語の新聞はどこで売ってますか。	eigo no shinbun wa doko uttemasu ka
I want to buy a/an/some . . .	…を買いたいのですが。	. . . o kaitai no desu ga
address book	住所録	jūshoroku
ball-point pen	ボールペン	bōrupen
book	本	hon
carbon paper	カーボン紙	kābonshi
cellophane tape	セロテープ	serotēpu
crayons	クレヨン	kureyon
dictionary	辞典	jiten
Japanese-English	和英	waei
English-Japanese	英和	eiwa
pocket dictionary	ポケット辞典	poketto jiten
drawing paper	画用紙	gayōshi
elastic bands	輪ゴム	wagomu
envelopes	封筒	fūtō
eraser	消しゴム	keshigomu
file	ファイル	fairu
fountain pen	万年筆	mannenhitsu
glue	糊	nori
grammar book	文法書	bunpōsho
guide book	案内書	annaisho
ink	インキ	inki
black/red/blue	黒／赤／青	kuro/aka/ao
labels	レッテル	retteru
magazine	雑誌	zasshi
map	地図	chizu
map of the town	市街地図	shigai chizu
road map	道路地図	dōrochizu

newspaper	新聞	shinbun
American/English	アメリカの/イギリスの	amerika no/igirisu no
notebook	ノート	nōto
note paper	便箋	binsen
paperback	文庫本	bunkobon
paper napkins	紙ナプキン	kaminapukin
paste	糊	nori
pen	ペン	pen
pencil	鉛筆	enpitsu
playing cards	トランプ	toranpu
postcards	葉書	hagaki
refill (for a pen)	カートリッジ	kātorijji
rubber bands	輪ゴム	wagomu
Scotch tape	セロテープ	serotēpu
sketching block	スケッチブック	suketchi bukku
stamps	切手	kitte
string	紐	himo
typewriter ribbon	タイプ用リボン	taipu yō ribon
typing paper	タイプ用紙	taipuyōshi
wrapping paper	包装紙	hōsoshi
Where's the guide-book section?	案内書売場はどこですか。	annaisho uriba wa doko desu ka
Where do you keep the English books?	英語の本はどこにありますか。	eigo no hon wa doko ni arimasu ka
Is there an English translation of . . . ?	…の英語訳がありますか。	. . . no eigoyaku ga arimasu ka

Here are some modern Japanese authors whose books are available in English translation.

Shusaku Endo
Yasunari Kawabata
Ichiro Kawasaki
Yukio Mishima
Soseki Natsume
Inazo Nitobe
Kakuzo Okakura
Daisetsu Suzuki
Junichiro Tanizaki

Chemist's (pharmacy)—Drugstore

Japanese chemists normally stock a range of goods as wide a the one you find at home. All major cities have excellent store and some offer round-the-clock service.

For reading ease, this section has been divided into two parts

1. Pharmaceutical—medicine, first-aid, etc.
2. Toiletry—toilet articles, cosmetics

General

Where's the nearest (all-night) chemist?	最寄りの（夜通しあいている）薬屋はどこですか。	moyori no (yodōshi aite iru) kusuriya wa doko desu ka
Can you recommend a good chemist?	良い薬屋を教えて下さい。	yoi kusuriya o oshiete kudasai
What time does the chemist open?	薬屋は何時に開きますか。	kusuriya wa nanji ni akimasu ka
When does the chemist close?	薬屋はいつ閉りますか。	kusuriya wa itsu shimari masu ka

Part 1—Pharmaceutical

I want something for . . .	…にきく薬が欲しいのですが。	. . . ni kiku kusuri ga hoshii no desu ga
a cold/a cough	風邪／咳	kaze/seki
hay-fever	枯草熱	karekusanetsu
a hangover	二日酔	futsukayoi
sunburn	日焼け	hiyake
travel sickness	旅行病	ryokōbyō
Can you make me up this prescription?	これを調剤して下さい。	kore o chōzai shite kudasai
Shall I wait?	お待ちしましょうか。	omachi shimashō ka
When shall I come back?	いつもらいに来たらいいですか。	itsu morai ni kitara ii desu ka

FOR DOCTOR, see page 162

Can I get it without a prescription?	これは処方箋がなくても頂けますか。	kore wa shohōsen ga nakute mo itadakemasu ka
Can I have a/an/some . . . ?	…を下さい。	. . . o kudasai
Alka Seltzer	アルカセルツアー	aruka serutsuā
antiseptic cream	消毒クリーム	shōdoku kurīmu
aspirin	アスピリン	asupirin
bandage	繃帯	hōtai
Band-Aids	絆創膏	bansōkō
chlorine tablets	塩素タブレット	enso taburetto
contraceptives	避妊薬	hininyaku
corn plasters	魚目膏薬	uonomekōyaku
cotton wool	脱脂綿	dasshimen
cough lozenges	咳止め錠剤	sekidome jōzai
diabetic lozenges	サッカリン錠剤	sakkarin jōzai
disinfectant	消毒薬	shōdokuyaku
ear drops	耳薬	mimigusuri
Elastoplast	絆創膏	bansōkō
eye drops	目薬	megusuri
first-aid kit	救急箱	kyūkyūbako
gargle	うがい薬	ugaigusuri
gauze	ガーゼ	gāze
insect lotion	虫刺され薬	mushisasare gusuri
insect repellent	殺虫剤	satchūzai
iodine	ヨードチンキ	yōdochinki
iron pills	鉄素剤	tetsusozai
laxative	通じ薬	tsūjigusuri
lint	リント布	rintofu
mouthwash	うがい薬	ugaigusuri
quinine tablets	キニーネ錠剤	kiniine jōzai
sanitary napkins	生理用ナプキン	sēriyo napukin
sedative	鎮静剤	chinseizai
sleeping pills	睡眠薬	suiminyaku
stomach pills	胃の薬	i no kusuri
thermometer	体温計	taionkē
throat lozenges	喉薬	nodogusuri
tissues	ティッシュペーパー	tishu pēpā
tranquilizers	精神安定剤	seishin antēzai
vitamin pills	ビタミン剤	bitaminzai
weight-reducing tablets	やせ薬	yasegusuri

Part 2—Toiletry

I'd like a/an/ some . . .	…を下さい。	. . . o kudasai
acne-cream	にきび用クリーム	nikibi yō kurīmu
after-shave lotion	アフターシエブローション	afutāshēbu rōshon
bath cubes	バスキューブ	basu kyūbu
bath essence	バスエッセンス	basu essensu
bath salts	バスソールト	basu sōruto
cream	クリーム	kurīmu
cleansing cream	クレンジングクリーム	kurenjingu kurīmu
cold cream	コールドクリーム	kōrudo kurīmu
cuticle cream	キューティクルクリーム	kyūtikuru kurīmu
foundation cream	ファンデーションクリーム	fandēshon kurīmu
hormone cream	ホルモンクリーム	horumon kurīmu
moisturizing cream	モイスチャライジングクリーム	moisucharaijingu kurīmu
night cream	ナイトクリーム	naito kurīmu
cuticle remover	キューティクルリムーバー	kyūtikuru rimūbā
deodorant	防臭剤	bōshūzai
spray/roll-on	スプレー／ロールオン	supurē/rōruon
eau de Cologne	オーデコロン	ōdekoron
emery board	つめやすり	tsumeyasuri
eye liner	アイライナー	airainā
eye pencil	アイペンシル	aipenshiru
eye shadow	アイシャドー	aishadō
face pack	パック	pakku
face powder	おしろい	oshiroi
foot cream	足のクリーム	ashi no kurīmu
hand cream	ハンドクリーム	hando kurīmu
Kleenex	クリーネックス	kurīnekkusu
lipstick	口紅	kuchibeni
lipstick brush	口紅ブラシ	kuchibeni burashi
make-up bag	化粧品入れ	keshōhin ire
make-up remover pads	化粧落としのパッド	keshōotoshi no paddo
nail brush	つめブラシ	tsume burashi
nail clippers	つめ切り	tsumekiri

SHOPPING-GUIDE

nail file	つめやすり	tsumeyasuri
nail lacquer	マニキュア	manikyua
nail lacquer remover	マニキュアリムーバー	manikyua rimūbā
nail polish	ネールポーリッシュ	nērupōrishu
nail scissors	つめ切りばさみ	tsumekiribasami
perfume	香水	kōsui
powder	おしろい	oshiroi
razor	かみそり	kamisori
razor blades	かみそりの刃	kamisori no ha
rouge	口紅	kuchibeni
safety pins	安全ピン	anzenpin
shampoo	シャンプー	shanpū
shaver	電気かみそり	denkikamisori
shaving brush	ひげそり用ブラシ	higesori yō burashi
shaving cream	ひげそり用クリーム	higesori yō kurīmu
shaving soap	ひげそり用石けん	higesori yō sekken
soap	石けん	sekken
sponge	スポンジ	suponji
sun-tan cream	サンタンクリーム	santan kurīmu
sun-tan oil	サンタンオイル	santan oiru
toilet bag	化粧袋	keshōbukuro
toilet paper	トイレットペーパー	toiretto pēpā
toothbrush	歯ブラシ	haburashi
toothpaste	ねり歯みがき	nerihamigaki
towel	手拭	tenugui
tweezers	毛抜き	kenuki

For your hair

brush	ヘアブラシ	heā burashi
colouring	毛染	kezome
comb	くし	kushi
curlers	カーラー	kārā
dye	染料	senryō
grips (bobby pins)	ヘアグリップ	heāgurippu
lacquer	ヘアラッカー	heārakkā
pins	ピン	pin
rollers	ローラ	rōrā
setting lotion	セットローション	setto rōshon

Clothing

If you want to buy something specific, prepare yourself i advance. Look at the list of clothing on page 113. Get some ide of the colour, material and size you want. They are all listed i the next few pages.

General

I'd like . . .	…を下さい。	. . . o kudasai
I want . . . for a 10-year-old boy.	10歳になる男の子に…が欲しいのですが。	ju-ssai ni naru otoko no ko . . . ga hoshii no desu ga
I want something like this.	何かこんな物が欲しいのですが。	nanika konna mono ga hoshii no desu ga
I like the one in the window.	ショーウィンドーに出ているのが気に入りました。	shō uindō ni dete iru no ga kiniirimashita
How much is that per metre?	一メートルに付きいくらですか。	ichi mētoru ni tsuki ikura desu ka

1 centimetre = 0.39 in.		1 inch = 2.54 cm.
1 metre = 39.37 in.		1 foot = 30.5 cm.
10 metres = 32.81 ft.		1 yard = 0.91 m.

Colour

I want something in . . .	…のが欲しいのですが。	. . . no ga hoshii no desu g
I want a darker shade.	もう少し色調の暗いのが欲しいのですが。	mō sukoshi shikichō no kurai no ga hoshii no desu g
I want something to match this.	これに合う物が欲しいのですが。	kore ni au mono ga hoshii n desu ga
I don't like the colour.	この色は気に入りません。	kono iro wa kiniirimasen

beige	ベージュ	bēju
black	黒	kuro
blue	青	ao
brown	茶色	chairo
cream	クリーム色	kurīmu-iro
crimson	深紅色	shinkōshoku
emerald	エメラルドグリーン	emerarudo gurīn
fawn	かげ色	kage-iro
gold	金色	kin-iro
green	緑色	midori-iro
grey	灰色	haiiro
mauve	ふじ色	fuji-iro
orange	だいだい色	daidai-iro
pink	桃色	momo-iro
purple	紫色	murasaki-iro
red	赤	aka
scarlet	緋色	hiiro
silver	銀色	gin-iro
tan	渋色	shibu-iro
white	白	shiro
yellow	黄色	kiiro

縞
(shima)

水玉模様
(mizutamamoyō)

格子縞
(kōshijima)

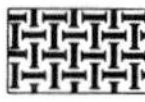
連続模様
(renzokumoyō)

Material

Have you anything . . . ?	…の物は何かありますか。	. . . no mono wa nanika arimasu ka
I want a cotton blouse.	木綿のブラウスを下さい。	momen no burausu o kudasai
Is that made here?	これは日本製ですか。	kore wa nihonsē desu ka
hand-made	手作りの	tezukuri no
imported	輸入の	yunyū no
I want something thinner.	もう少し薄手の物が欲しいのですが。	mō sukoshi usude no mono ga hoshii no desu ga

Have you any better quality?	もっと上等の物はありませんか。	motto jōtō no mono wa arimasen ka
What's it made of?	生地は何ですか。	kiji wa nan desu ka

It may be made of . . .

camel-hair	ラクダの毛	rakuda no ke
chiffon	絹モスリン	kinu mosurin
corduroy	コールテン	kōruten
cotton	木綿	momen
felt	フェルト	feruto
flannel	フラノ	furano
gabardine	ギャバジン	gyabajin
lace	レース	rēsu
leather	革	kawa
linen	リンネル	rinneru
nylon	ナイロン	nairon
pique	ピケ	pike
poplin	ポプリン	popurin
rayon	レーヨン	rēyon
rubber	ゴム	gomu
satin	サテン	saten
serge	サージ	sāji
silk	絹	kinu
suede	スエード革	suēdo gawa
towelling	タオル地	taoruji
tulle	チュール	chūru
tweed	ツイード	tsuīdo
velvet	ビロード	birōdo
wool	羊毛	yōmō
worsted	ウーステッド	ūsuteddo

Size

My size is 38.	私のサイズは38です。	watashi no saizu wa sanj hachi desu
Our sizes are different at home. Could you measure me?	国によってサイズが違いますから計って下さい。	kuni ni yotte saizu ga chiga masu kara hakatte kudasai
I don't know the Japanese sizes.	日本のサイズは知りません。	nihon no saizu wa shirimase

In that case, look at the charts on the next page.

This is your size

Ladies

Dresses/suits						
American	10	12	14	16	18	20
British	32	34	36	38	40	42
Japanese	9	11	13	15	17	19

Stockings					
American / British	8	8½	9½	9½	10
Japanese	20	21	22	23	24

Shoes				
American	6	7	8	9
British	4½	5	6½	7
Japanese	22	22½	24	24½

Gentlemen

Suits/overcoats						
American / British	36	38	40	42	44	46
Japanese	90	95	100	105	110	115

Shirts				
American / British	15	16	17	18
Japanese	38	41	43	45

Shoes									
American / British	5	6	7	8	8½	9	9½	10	11
Japanese	23	24	25	26	26½	27	27½	28	29

A good fit?

Can I try it on?	これを試していいですか。	kore o tameshite ii desu ka
Where's the fitting room?	試着室はどこですか。	shichakushitsu wa doko desu ka
Is there a mirror?	鏡はどこですか。	kagami wa doko desu ka
Does it fit?	ぴったりですか	pittari desu ka

FOR NUMBERS, see page 175

SHOPPING–GUIDE

It fits very well.	ぴったり合います。	pittari aimasu
It doesn't fit.	合いません。	aimasen
It's too . . .	…過ぎます。	. . . sugimasu
short/long/tight/ loose	短／長／きつ／ゆる	mijika/naga/kitsu/yuru
How long will it take to alter?	直すのにどの位掛かりますか。	naosu noni dono kurai kakarimasu ka

Shoes

I'd like a pair of . . .	…を一足下さい。	. . . o issoku kudasai
shoes/sandals/boots	靴／サンダル／ブーツ	kutsu/sandaru/būtsu
These are too . . .	…過ぎます。	. . . sugimasu
narrow/wide	きつ／ひろ	kitsu/hiro
large/small	大き／小さ	ōki/chīsa
Do you have a larger size?	もっと大きなサイズはありませんか。	motto ōki na saizu wa arimasen ka
I want a smaller size.	もっと小さなサイズをお願いします。	motto chīsa na saizu o o-negai shimasu
Do you have the same in . . . ?	…で同じ物がありますか。	. . . de onaji mono ga arimasu ka
brown/beige	茶色／ベージュ	chairo/bēju
black/white	黒／白	kuro/shiro

Shoes worn out? Here's the key to getting them fixed again. . .

Can you repair these shoes?	この靴を直して下さい。	kono kutsu o naoshite kudasai
Can you stitch this?	これを縫ってください。	kore o nutte kudasai
I want new soles and heels.	靴底とかかとを替えたいのですが。	kutsuzoko to kakato o kaetai no desu ga
When will they be ready?	いつ出来ますか。	itsu dekimasu ka

lothes and accessories

vould like a/an/ me . . .	…を下さい。	. . . o kudasai
10rak	アノラック	anorakku
ıthing cap	水泳帽	suiēbō
ıthing suit	海水着	kaisuigi
ıth robe	部屋着	heyagi
kini	ビキニ	bikini
azer	ブレザーコート	burezā kōto
ouse	ブラウス	burausu
olero	ボレロ	borero
ow tie	蝶ネクタイ	chōnekutai
'a	ブラジャー	burajā
'aces (Br.)	ズボン吊り	zubontsuri
ıp	帽子	bōshi
ıpe	ケープ	kēpu
ırdigan	カーディガン	kādigan
oat	上衣	uwagi
ostume	スーツ	sūtsu
nner jacket	タキシード	takishīdo
'ess	ドレス	doresu
'essing gown	部屋着	heyagi
vening dress (woman's)	イヴニングドレス	ibuningu doresu
ungarees	ダンガリーズボン	dangarī zubon
ock	ドレス	doresu
ır coat	毛皮コート	kegawa kōto
ırdle	ガードル	gādoru
loves	手袋	tebukuro
andkerchief	ハンカチ	hankachi
at	帽子	bōshi
ousecoat	部屋着	heyagi
ıcket	ジャケット	jaketto
ans	ジーパン	jīpan
rsey	ジャージー	jājī
ımper(Br.)	ジャンパー	janpā
imono	着物	kimono
nickers	半ズボン	han zubon
ngerie	下着	shitagi
ıackintosh	レインコート	rein kōto
ecktie	ネクタイ	nekutai
ightdress	寝間着	nemaki

overcoat	オーバーコート	ōbā kōto
petticoat	ペティコート	petikōto
pullover	プルオーバー	puruōbā
pyjamas	パジャマ	pajama
raincoat	レインコート	rein kōto
robe	ワンピース	wanpīsu
rubber boots	ゴムの長靴	gomu no nagagutsu
sandals	サンダル	sandaru
scarf	スカーフ	sukāfu
shirt	ワイシャツ	waishatsu
shoes	靴	kutsu
shorts(Br.)	ショートパンツ	shōto pantsu
skirt	スカート	sukāto
slacks	スラックス	surakkusu
slip	スリップ	surippu
slippers	スリッパー	surippā
sneakers	ズック靴	zukku gutsu
socks	靴下	kutsushita
sports jacket	スポーツ用ジャケット	supōtsu-yō jaketto
stockings	靴下	kutsushita
suit (men's)	背広	sebiro
suspenders	ズボン吊り	zubontsuri
sweater	セーター	sēta
T-shirt	半そでシャツ	hansode shatsu
tennis shoes	テニス靴	tenisu gutsu
tie	ネクタイ	nekutai
top coat	トッパー	toppā
trousers	ズボン	zubon
underpants (men)	パンツ	pantsu

belt	ベルト	beruto
buckle	バックル	bakkuru
button	ボタン	botan
collar	えり	eri
cuffs	カフス	kafusu
elastic	ゴム	gomu
hem	ふち	fuchi
lapel	返しえり	kaeshieri
lining	裏	ura
pocket	ポケット	poketto
ribbon	リボン	ribon
sleeve	そで	sode
zip(per)	ジッパー	jippā

Electrical appliances and accessories—Records

Electric current in Japan is 100–110 volt, AC, but the cycles are different depending on the regions. The country's eastern half including Tokyo has 50 cycles, while the western half is on a 60-cycle basis. The dividing line is situated near Shizuoka. Outlets are American style.

I want a plug for this . . .	これを使うための差し込みが欲しいのですが。	kore o tsukau tame no sashikomi ga hoshiino desu ga
Have you a battery for this . . . ?	これの電池を下さい。	kore no denchi o kudasai
This is broken. Can you repair it?	これはこわれています。修理して頂けますか。	kore wa kowarete imasu. shūri shite itadakemasu ka
When will it be ready?	いつ出来ますか。	itsu dekimasu ka
I'd like a/an/some . . .	…を下さい。	. . . o kudasai
adaptor	アダプター	adaputā
amplifier	アンプ	anpu
battery	電池	denchi
cassette	カセット	kasetto
clock	時計	tokē
wall clock	壁時計	kabedokē
electronic calculator	電卓	dentaku
food mixer	ミキサー	mikisā
hair-dryer	ヘアドライアー	heā doraiyā
headset	ヘッドフォーン	heddofōn
iron	アイロン	airon
microphone	マイク	maiku
percolator	コーヒー沸し	kōhī wakashi
plug	差し込み	sashikomi
radio	ラジオ	rajio
car radio	自動車用ラジオ	jidōsha-yō rajio
portable radio	ポータブルラジオ	pōtaburu rajio
record	レコード	rekōdo
record player	レコードプレーヤ	rekōdo purēyā
portable record player	ポータブルレコードプレーヤ	pōtaburu rekōdo purēyā
shaver	電気かみそり	denkikamisori
speakers	スピーカー	supīkā

tape recorder	テープレコーダー	tēpu rekōdā
cassette tape recorder	カセット式テープレコーダー	kasetto-shiki tēpu rekōdā
portable tape recorder	ポータブルテープレコーダー	pōtaburu tēpu rekōdā
television	テレビ	terebi
colour television	カラーテレビ	karā terebi
portable television	ポータブルテレビ	pōtaburu terebi
toaster	トースター	tōsutā

Record shop

Have you any records by . . . ?	…のレコードがありますか。	. . . no rekōdo ga arimasu ka
Can I listen to this record?	このレコードを試聴出来ますか。	kono rekōdo o shichō deki masu ka
I want a new needle.	新しい針が欲しいのですか。	atarashii hari ga hoshiino desu ga

L.P.	エルピー	erupī
33/45 rpm	33／45回転	san-jū-san/yon-jū-go kaiten
mono/stereo	モノ／ステレオ	mono/sutereo

classical music	クラシック音楽	kurasshikku ongaku
folk music	民よう	minyō
instrumental music	器楽	kigaku
jazz	ジャズ	jazu
light music	軽音楽	kēongaku
orchestral music	管弦楽	kangengaku
pop music	ポップミュジック	poppu myūjikku

Here are the names of a few popular recording artists known throughout Japan.

Mina Aoe
Blue Comets
Naomi Chiaki
Keiko Fuji
Kazuo Funaki
Akira Fuse
Mari Henmi
Hide & Rosanna
Mieko Hirota
Ayumi Ishida
Yukari Ito
Hibari Misora
Harumi Miyako
Shinichi Mori
Chiyo Okamura
Peter
Teruhiko Saigo
Masao Sen
The Spiders
Yoichi Sugawara
Toi et Moi

SHOPPING–GUIDE

Equipment

Here we're concerned with the equipment you may need when camping, picnicking or on excursions — or for just one of those odd situations when one needs something he never would have thought of. . .

I'd like a/an/some . . .	…を下さい。	. . . o kudasai
axe	おの	ono
bottle-opener	栓抜き	sennuki
bucket	バケツ	baketsu
butane gas	ブタンガス	butangasu
camp bed	キャンプベッド	kyanpubeddo
camping equipment	キャンピング装具	kyanpingu sōgu
can opener	罐切り	kankiri
candles	ろうそく	rōsoku
chair	椅子	isu
folding chair	折りたたみ椅子	oritatami isu
compass	磁石	jishaku
corkscrew	コルク抜き	korukunuki
crockery	瀬戸物	setomono
cutlery	食卓用ナイフ類	shokutaku-yō naifurui
deck chair	デッキチェアー	dekkichea
first-aid kit	救急箱	kyūkyūbako
fishing tackle	釣用具	tsuriyōgu
flashlight	懐中電灯	kaichūdentō
frying pan	フライパン	furaipan
groundsheet	防水敷布	bōsuishikifu
hammer	かなづち	kanazuchi
hammock	ハンモック	hanmokku
haversack	雑のう	zatsunō
ice-bag	氷袋	kōribukuro
kerosene	灯油	tōyu
kettle	やかん	yakan
knapsack	ナップサック	nappusakku
lamp	ランプ	ranpu
lantern	提灯	chōchin
matches	マッチ	matchi
mattress	マットレス	mattoresu
mosquito net	蚊帳	kaya
pail	バケツ	baketsu

paraffin	灯油	tōyu
penknife	ペンナイフ	pennaifu
picnic case	遠足袋	ensokubukuro
pressure cooker	圧力がま	atsuryokugama
primus stove	プリムスストーブ	purimusu sutōbu
rope	なわ	nawa
rucksack	リュックサック	ryukkusakku
saucepan	シチューなべ	shichū nabe
scissors	はさみ	hasami
screwdriver	ねじ回し	nejimawashi
sheath-knife	ナイフ	naifu
sleeping bag	寝袋	nebukuro
stewpan	シチューなべ	shichū nabe
stove	ストーブ	sutōbu
table	テーブル	tēburu
folding table	折りたたみテーブル	oritatami tēburu
tent	テント	tento
tent peg	テントの杭	tento no kui
tent-pole	テントの支柱	tento no shichū
thermos flask (bottle)	まほうびん	mahōbin
tin-opener	罐切り	kankiri
tongs	火箸	hibashi
tool kit	道具	dōgu
torch	懐中電灯	kaichūdentō
vacuum flask	まほうびん	mahōbin
water carrier	携帯用水タンク	keitai-yō mizutanku

Crockery

beakers	コップ	koppu
cups	茶碗	chawan
mugs	ヂョッキ	jokki
plates	皿	sara
saucers	受皿	ukezara

Cutlery

forks	フオーク	fōku
knives	ナイフ	naifu
spoons	スプーン	supūn
teaspoons	ティースプーン	tīsupūn
(made of) plastic	プラスチックの	purasutikku no
(made of) stainless steel	ステンレスの	sutenresu no

SHOPPING – GUIDE

Men's hairdressing (barber)

I don't speak much Japanese.	余り日本語を話しません。	amari nihongo o hanashimasen
I'm in a terrible hurry.	とても急いでいます。	totemo isoide imasu
I want a haircut, please.	散髪，お願いします。	sanpatsu. onegai shimasu
I'd like a shave.	ひげをそってください。	hige o sotte kudasai
Don't cut it too short.	余り短く刈らないで下さい。	amari mijikaku karanai de kudasai
Scissors only, please.	はさみでお願いします。	hasami de o-negai shimasu
A razor-cut, please.	レザーカットでお願いします。	rezākatto de o-negai shimasu
Don't use the clippers.	バリカンは使わないで下さい。	barikan wa tsukawanai de kudasai
Just a trim, please.	ざっとお願いします。	zāto o-negai shimasu
That's enough off.	それで十分です。	sore de jūbun desu
A little more off the . . .	…をもう少し刈ってください。	. . . o mō sukoshi katte kudasai
back	うしろ	ushiro
neck	襟首	erikubi
sides	両側	ryōgawa
top	てっぺん	teppen
I don't want any cream.	クリームは入りません。	kurīmu wa irimasen
Would you please trim my . . . ?	…を少し刈り込んで下さい。	. . . o sukoshi karikon de kudasai
beard	あごひげ	agohige
moustache	口ひげ	kuchihige
sideboards (side-burns)	頬ひげ	hoohige
Thank you. That's fine.	ありがとう，これでいいです。	arigatō. korede ii desu
How much do I owe you?	いくらですか。	ikura desu ka

FOR TIPPING, see inside back-cover

Ladies' hairdressing

Is there a beauty salon in the hotel?	ホテルの中に美容院がありますか。	hoteru no naka ni biyōin ga arimasu ka
Can I make an appointment for sometime on Tuesday?	火曜日の適当な時間に予約がとれますか。	kayōbi no tekitō na jikan ni yoyaku ga toremasu ka
I'd like it cut and shaped . . .	…にして下さい。	. . . ni shite kudasai
with a fringe	切下げ前髪	kirisage maegami
with ringlets	巻き毛	makige
with waves	ウエーブ	uēbu
in a bun	シニヨン・スタイル	shinion sutairu
I want a . . .	…をお願いします。	. . . o o-negai shimasu
bleach	脱色	dasshoku
colour rinse	カラーリンス	karārinsu
dye	染料	senryō
perm(anent)	パーマ	pāma
shampoo and set	シャンプーとセット	shanpû to setto
tint	つやだし	tsuyadashi
touch up	手直し	tenaoshi
the same colour	同じ色	onaji iro
a darker colour	もっと濃い色	motto koi iro
a lighter colour	もっと薄い色	motto usui iro
auburn/blond/brunette	とび色／ブロンド／ブルーネット	tobi-iro/burondo/burūnetto
I want a . . .	…をお願いします。	. . . o onegai shimasu
manicure/pedicure/facepack	マニキュア／ペディキュア／パック	manikyua/pedikyua/pakku

FOR TIPPING, see inside back-cover

SHOPPING – GUIDE

eweller's—Watchmaker's

an you repair this 'atch?	この時計を修理して頂けますか。	kono tokē o shūri shite itadakemasu ka
ne . . . is broken.	…がこわれました。	. . . ga kowaremashita
ass/spring/strap	ガラス／ぜんまい／バンド	garasu/zenmai/bando
want this watch eaned.	この時計を分解掃除してください。	kono tokē o bunkaisōji shite kudasai
/hen will it be eady?	いつ出来上がりますか。	itsu deki agarimasu ka
ould I see that, lease?	それを見せて下さい。	sore o misete kudasai
m just looking round.	見せてもらっている所です。	misete moratte iru tokoro desu
want a small present or . . .	…へのちょっとしたおみやげを捜しています。	. . . eno chotto shita omiyage o sagashite imasu
don't want any-ning too expensive.	余り高価な物は入りません。	amari kōka-na mono wa irimasen
want something . . .	何か…物が欲しいのですが。	nanika . . . mono ga hoshii no desu ga
etter/cheaper/ simpler	もっと良い／もっと安い／もっと簡単な	motto yoi/motto yasui/ motto kantan na
Have you anything in old?	何か金の物がありますか。	nani ka kin no mono ga arimasu ka
s this real silver?	これは本当の銀ですか。	kore wa hontō no gin desu ka

f it's made of gold, ask:

How many carats is his?	何カラットですか。	nan karatto desu ka

Japan is a producer of world-famous cultured pearls and offers a far greater variety of them than anywhere else in the world. They're among the best bets at a Japanese jeweller's.

When you go to a jeweller's, you've probably got some idea what you want beforehand. Find out what the article is made and then look up the Japanese name for the article itself in th following lists.

What's it made of?

amber	琥珀	kohaku
amethyst	アメジスト	amejisuto
chromium	クローム	kurōmu
copper	銅	dō
coral	珊瑚	sango
crystal	水晶	suishō
cut-glass	カットグラス	katto gurasu
diamond	ダイヤ	daiya
ebony	黒檀	kokutan
emerald	エメラルド	emerarudo
enamel	エナメル	enameru
glass	ガラス	garasu
gold	金	kin
gold-leaf	金箔	kinpaku
ivory	象牙	zōge
jade	翡翠	hisui
onyx	縞瑪瑙	shimameno
pearl	真珠	shinju
pewter	ピューター	pyūtā
platinum	プラチナ	purachina
ruby	ルビー	rubī
sapphire	サファイア	safaia
silver	銀	gin
silver-plate	銀メッキ	ginmekki
stainless steel	ステンレス	sutenresu
topaz	黄玉，トッパーズ	kōgyoku, toppāzu
turquoise	トルコ石	torukoishi

What is it?

I'd like a/an/ some . . .	…を下さい	. . . o kudasai
bracelet	腕輪	udewa
brooch	ブローチ	burōchi
chain	鎖	kusari
charm	お守り	omamori
cigarette case	シガレットケース	shigaretto kesu
cigarette lighter	ライター	raita
clock	置時計	okidokē
cross	十字架	jujika
cuff-links	カフスボタン	kafusu botan
cutlery	食卓用ナイフ類	shokutaku-yō naifurui
earrings	イアリング	iaringu
jewel box	宝石箱	hōsekibako
manicure set	マニキュアセット	manikyua setto
mechanical pencil	シャープペンシル	shāpu penshiru
necklace	ネックレス	nekkuresu
pendant	ペンダント	pendanto
pin	ピン	pin
powder compact	コンパクト	konpakuto
propelling pencil	シャープペンシル	shāpu penshiru
ring	指輪	yubiwa
engagement ring	婚約指輪	konyaku yubiwa
wedding ring	結婚指輪	kekkon yubiwa
rosary	ロザリオ	rozario
silverware	銀器	ginki
strap	バンド	bando
chain strap	鎖製バンド	kusarisei bando
leather strap	革バンド	kawa bando
watch strap	時計のバンド	tokē no bando
tie-clip	ネクタイ止め	nekutai dome
tie-pin	ネクタイピン	nekutai pin
vanity case	化粧道具入れ	keshōdōguire
watch	時計	tokē
pocket watch	懐中時計	kaichūdokē
with a second-hand	秒針付き	byōshintsuki
wrist-watch	腕時計	udedokē

Laundry—Dry cleaning

If your hotel doesn't have its own laundry/dry cleaning service ask the porter:

Where's the nearest laundry?	最寄りの洗濯屋はどこですか。	moyori no sentakuya wa doko desu ka
I want these clothes . . .	この服を…下さい。	kono fuku o . . . kudasai
cleaned	クリーニングして	kuriningu shite
pressed	プレスして	puresu shite
ironed	アイロンして	airon shite
washed	洗って	aratte
When will it be ready?	いつ出来ますか。	itsu dekimasu ka
I need it . . .	…入ります。	. . . irimasu
today	今日中に	kyōjū ni
tonight	今晩までに	konban made ni
tomorrow	明日までに	asu made ni
before Friday	金曜日までに	kinyōbi made ni
I want it as soon as possible.	出来るだけ早くお願いします。	dekiru dake hayaku onegai shimasu
Can you . . . this?	これを…頂けますか。	kore o . . . itadakemasu ka
mend/patch/stitch	繕って／つぎあてして／かがって	tsukurotte/tsugiate shite/kagatte
Can you sew on this button?	このボタンを付けて頂けますか。	kono botan o tsukete itadake masu ka
Can you get this stain out?	このしみはとれますか。	kono shimi wa toremasu ka
Can this be invisibly mended?	目立たぬように繕って頂けますか。	medatanu yō ni tsukurotte itadake-masu ka
This isn't mine.	これは私のではありません。	kore wa watashino de wa arimasen
Where's my laundry? You promised it for today.	私の洗濯物はどこですか。今日までに出来る事になっているのですが。	watashi no sentakumono wa doko desu ka. kyō made ni dekiru koto ni natte iru no desu ga

hotography—Cameras

he basic still and home-movie exposures are given in English the instructions with the roll.

want an inexpensive amera.	安いカメラが欲しいのですが。	yasui kamera ga hoshiino desu ga
how me that one in ne window.	ショーウインドーに出ているあれを見せて下さい。	shō uindō ni deteiru are o misete kudasai

Films

'd like a . . .	…が欲しいのですが。	. . . ga hoshii no desu ga
ilm for this camera	このカメラ用のフィルム	kono kamera yō no fuirumu
20 (6 × 6) film	6 × 6のフィルム	roku roku no fuirumu
26 (26 × 26) film	26 × 26のフィルム	ni-jū-roku ni-jū-roku no fuirumu
27 (4 × 4) film	4 × 4のフィルム	yon yon no fuirumu
35 (24 × 36) film	24 × 36のフィルム	ni-jū-shi san-jū-roku no fuirumu
26 Instamatic	126インスタマチック	hyaku-ni-jyū-roku insuta machiku
3mm film	8ミリフィルム	hachi miri fuirumu
uper 8	スーパー8	sūpā eito
6mm film	16ミリフィルム	jū-roku miri fuirumu
35mm film	35ミリフィルム	san-jū-go miri fuirumu
520 (6 × 6) roll film	細軸ブロニー判のフィルム	hosojiku buronī ban no fuirumu
20/36 exposures	20／36巻	ni-jū/san-jū-roku-maki
his size	このサイズ	kono saizu
his ASA/DIN number	このフィルム感度	kono fuirumu kando
black and white	白黒	shirokuro
colour	カラー	karā
colour negative	カラーネガティブ	karā negatibu
colour reversal	カラーリバーサル	karā ribāsaru
colour slide (transparency)	カラースライド	karā suraido
artificial light type	タングステンタイプ	tangusuten taipu
daylight type	デイライトタイプ	deiraito taipu
fast/fine grain	高感度／微粒子フィルム	kōkando/biryūshi fuirumu
Does this price include processing?	現像代も入っていますか。	genzōdai mo haitte imasu ka

FOR NUMBERS, see page 175

Processing

How much do you charge for developing?	現像代はいくらですか。	genzōdai wa ikura desu ka
I want . . . prints of each negative.	このネガを…枚づつプリントして欲しいのですが。	kono nega o . . . mai zut purinto shite hoshii no des ga
Will you enlarge this, please?	これを引伸して頂けますか。	kore o hikinobashite itadak masu ka

Accessories

I want a/an/ some . . .	…を下さい。	. . . o kudasai
cable release	シャッターレリーズ	shattā rerīzu
exposure meter	露出計	roshutsukē
flash bulbs	フラッシュバルブ	furasshu barubu
flash cubes	フラッシュキューブ	furasshu kyūbu
for black and white	白黒用	shirokuro yō
for colour	カラー用	karā yō
filter	フィルター	firutā
red/yellow	赤／黄色	aka/kiiro
ultra-violet	紫外線	shigaisen
lens	レンズ	renzu
lens cap	レンズキャップ	renzu kyappu
lens cleaners	レンズクリーナー	renzu kurīnā
tripod	三脚	sankyaku
zoom lens	ズームレンズ	zūmu renzu

Broken

This camera doesn't work. Can you repair it?	このカメラはこわれています。修理出来ますか。	kono kamera wa kowarete imasu. shūri dekimasu ka
The film is jammed.	フィルムが動きません。	fuirumu ga ugokimasen
There's something wrong with the . . .	…がどこか悪いようです。	. . . ga dokoka warui yō desu
exposure counter	露出計	roshutsukē
film winder	フィルムワインダー	fuirumu waindā
lightmeter	ライトメーター	raito mēta
rangefinder	レンジファインダー	renji faindā
shutter	シャッター	shattā

'rovisions

lere's a list of basic food and drink that you might want on a icnic or for the occasional meal at home.

d like a/an/ ome . . .	…が欲しいのですが。	. . . ga hoshiino desu ga
pples	りんご	ringo
ananas	バナナ	banana
scuits (Br.)	ビスケット	bisuketto
'read	パン	pan
utter	バター	batā
ake	ケーキ	kēki
heese	チーズ	chīzu
hocolate	チョコレート	chokorēto
offee	コーヒー	kōhī
old meat	冷肉	reiniku
ookies	ビスケット	bisuketto
ooking fat	料理用油	ryōri-yō abura
rackers	クラッカー	kurakkā
risps (potato chips)	ポテトチップ	poteto chippu
ucumbers	きゅうり	kyūri
ankfurters	ウィンナーソーセージ	winnā sōsēji
am	ハム	hamu
amburgers	ハンバーガー	hanbāgā
e-cream	アイスクリーム	aisukurīmu
monade	レモネード	remonēdo
mons	レモン	remon
ttuce	レタス	retasu
ver sausage	レバーソーセージ	rebā sōsēji
ncheon meat	コンビーフ類	conbīfu rui
ilk	ミルク	miruku
ustard	からし	karashi
range squash (drink)	オレンジスカッシュ	orenji sukasshu
ranges	オレンジ	orenji
até	パテ	pate
epper	胡椒	koshō
ickles	漬物	tsukemono
ork	豚肉	butaniku
otatoes	じゃがいも	jagaimo
olls	ロールパン	rōru pan
alad	サラダ	sarada
alami	サラミ	sarami

sandwiches	サンドウィッチ	sandoittchi
sausages	ソーセージ	sōsēji
spaghetti	スパゲッティ	supageti
sugar	砂糖	satō
sweets	菓子	kashi
tea	紅茶	kōcha
tomatoes	トマト	tomato

And don't forget . . .

a bottle opener	栓抜き	sennuki
a corkscrew	コルク抜き	korukunuki
matches	マッチ	matchi
(paper) napkins	紙ナプキン	kami napukin
a tin (can) opener	罐切り	kankiri

Weights and measures

1 kilogram or kilo (kg) = 1000 grams (g)

100 g = 3.5 oz.	½ kg = 1.1 lb.
200 g = 7.0 oz.	1 kg = 2.2 lb.

1 oz. = 28.35 g
1 lb. = 453.60 g

1 litre (l) = 0.88 imp. quarts = 1.06 U.S. quarts

1 imp. quart = 1.14 l	1 U.S. quart = 0.95 l
1 imp. gallon = 4.55 l	1 U.S. gallon = 3.8 l

barrel	たる	taru
box	箱	hako
can	カン	kan
carton	ボール箱	bōrubako
crate	かご	kago
jar	つぼ	tsubo
packet	包み	tsutsumi
tin	カン	kan
tube	チューブ	chūbu

Souvenirs

It need hardly be said in this section that Japanese electronic and optical products can be bought at bargain prices in their country of origin. Other souvenir articles considered good buys in Japan are:

bamboo products	竹製品	takesēhin
brocades	錦	nishiki
cigarette lighters	ライター	raita
cultured pearls	真珠	shinju
cutlery	食卓用ナイフ類	shokutakuyō naifurui
damask	象嵌	zōgan
dolls	人形	ningyō
fans	扇子	sensu
fishing rods and reels	釣道具	tsuridōgu
folkcrafts	民芸品	mingeihin
handbags	ハンドバック	handobaggu
hanging-picture rolls	掛物	kakemono
kimono	着物	kimono
lacquerware	塗物	nurimono
manicure sets	マニキュアセット	manikyua setto
music boxes	オルゴール	orugōru
painted screens	屏風	byōbu
paper products	紙製品	kamisēhin
porcelains	陶磁器	tōjiki
silks	絹	kinu
swords	刀剣類	tōkenrui
toys	おもちゃ	omocha
woodblock prints	木版画	mokuhanga

Tobacconist's

As elsewhere, cigarettes are generally referred to by their brand names. The best-known Japanese cigarettes are *Hi-Lite* and *Seven star*.

Buying

Give me a/an/ some . . . please.	…を下さい。	. . . o kudasai
box of . . .	…を一箱	. . . o hito-hako
cigar	葉巻	hamaki
cigarette case	たばこ入れ	tabakoire
cigarette holder	パイプ	paipu
cigarette lighter	ライター	raitā
flints	ライターの石	raitā no ishi
lighter	ライター	raitā
lighter fluid/gas	ライター用オイル／ガス	raitā-yō oiru/gasu
refill for a lighter	詰め替え	tsumekae
matches	マッチ	matchi
packet of cigarettes	たばこ一箱	tabako hito-hako
packet of . . .	…を一箱	. . . o hito-hako
pipe	パイプ	paipu
pipe tobacco	パイプたばこ	paipu tabako
pipe cleaners	パイプクリーナー	paipu kurīnā
tobacco pouch	たばこ入れ	tabakoire
wick	芯	shin
Have you any . . . ?	…がありますか。	. . . ga arimasu ka
American cigarettes	アメリカのたばこ	amerika no tabako
English cigarettes	イギリスのたばこ	igirisu no tabako
matches	マッチ	matchi
menthol cigarettes	はっかたばこ	hakka tabako
I'll take two packets.	二箱下さい。	futa-hako kudasai
I'd like a carton.	カートン一つ下さい。	kāton hitotsu kudasai

filter-tipped	フィルター付き	firutā tsuki
without filter	フィルターなし	firutā nashi

While we're on the subject of cigarettes, suppose you want to offer somebody one?

Would you like a cigarette?	たばこをいかがですか。	tabako o ikaga desu ka
Have one of mine.	私のたばこをどうぞ。	watashi no tabako o dōzo
Try one of these. They're very mild.	ちょっとこれを吸って御覧なさい。とてもまろやかですよ。	chotto kore o sutte goran-nasai. totemo maroyaka desu yo
They're a bit strong.	ちょっと強いです。	chotto tsuyoi desu

And if somebody offers you one?

Thank you.	どうもありがとう。	dōmo arigatō
No, thanks.	いいえ結構です。	iie kekko desu
I don't smoke.	私はたばこを吸いません。	watashi wa tabako o suimasen
I've given it up.	私は止めました。	watashi wa yamemashita

Your money: banks—currency

Money and traveller's cheques can be exchanged only at authorizec currency exchanges, such as leading Western-style hotels, bank and top shops catering to foreign visitors. At larger places there i sure to be someone who speaks English. Remember to tak your passport with you, since you may need it.

Hours

Banks are open from 9 a.m. through 3 p.m. on weekdays, and from 9 a.m. through noon on Saturdays. All banks are closed on Sundays, but Tokyo Airport's bank is open 24 hours a day the year round.

Monetary unit

The Japanese monetary system is based on the *yen*. The word *yen* is abbreviated as ¥.

The first four items listed below are coins, the others are notes. 100 yen can be a nickel coin or a note.

Value	Coin/note
1 yen	aluminium coin
5 yen	brass coin
10 yen	copper coin
50 yen	nickel coin
100 yen	nickel coin
500 yen	banknote
1,000 yen	banknote
5,000 yen	banknote
10,000 yen	banknote

Before going

Where's the nearest bank?	最寄りの銀行はどこですか。	moyori no ginkō wa doko desu ka
Where can I cash a traveller's cheque (check)?	トラベラーチェックをどこで現金に替えられますか。	toraberā cheku o doko de genkin ni kaeraremasu ka
Where's the American Express?	アメリカンエックスプレスはどこですか。	amerikan ekkusupuresu wa doko desu ka

Inside

I want to change some dollars.	ドルを替えたいのですが。	doru o kaetai no desu ga
I'd like to change some pounds.	ポンドを替えたいのですが。	pondo o kaetai no desu ga
Here's my passport.	これが私のパスポートです。	kore ga watashi no pasupōto desu
What's the exchange rate?	交換レートはいくらですか。	kōkan rēto wa ikura desu ka
What rate of commission do you charge?	コミッションはいくらですか。	komisshon wa ikura desu ka
Can you cash a personal cheque?	銀行小切手を現金に替えられますか。	ginkō-kogitte o genkin ni kaeraremasu ka
How long will it take to clear the cheque?	小切手をクリアするにはどの位時間が掛かりますか。	kogitte o kuriā suru ni wa dono kurai jikan ga kakarimasu ka
Can you cable my bank in . . . ?	…の私の銀行に電報を打って頂けますか。	. . . no watashi no ginkō ni denpō o utte itadakemasu ka
I have . . .	…があります。	. . . ga arimasu
a letter of credit	信用状	shinyōjō
an introduction from . . .	…の紹介状	. . . no shōkaijō
a credit card	クレジットカード	kurejito kādo
I'm expecting some money from the U.S. Has it arrived yet?	アメリカから現金が来る事になっていますが着きましたか。	amerika kara genkin ga kuru koto ni natte imasu ga tsukimashita ka

Depositing

I want to credit this to my account.	これを私の口座に入れて下さい。	kore o watashi no kōza ni irete kudasai
I want to credit this to Mr. Simon's account.	この金額をシモンさんの口座に入れて下さい。	kono kingaku o simon san no kōza ni irete kudasai
Where should I sign?	どこにサインしたらいいですか。	doko ni sain shitara ii desu ka

Currency converter

In a world of fluctuating currencies, we can offer no more than this do-it-yourself chart. You can get a card showing current exchange rates from banks, travel agencies and tourist offices. Why not fill in this chart, too, for handy reference?

Yen	£	$
10		
50		
100		
500		
1,000		
5,000		
10,000		
50,000		
100,000		
500,000		
1,000,000		
5,000,000		

FOR NUMBERS, see page 175

ost office

ost offices are indicated by a red and white double-capped sign. Mail boxes are painted red. Business hours are from 9 .m. through 5 p.m. without interruption.

Vhere's the nearest ost office?	最寄りの郵便局はどこですか。	moyori no yūbinkyoku wa doko desu ka
Vhat time does the ost office open?	郵便局は何時に開きますか。	yūbinkyoku wa nanji ni akimasu ka
Vhen does the post ffice close?	郵便局はいつ閉りますか。	yūbinkyoku wa itsu shimari-masu ka
Vhat window should go to for stamps?	切手はどの窓口ですか。	kitte wa dono madoguchi desu ka
At which counter can cash an international noney order?	外国為替はどのカウンターですか。	gaikokukawase wa dono kauntā desu ka
want . . . 50-yen stamps and . . . 100-yen stamps.	50円切手を…枚と100円切手を…枚下さい。	go-jūen kitte o . . . mai to hyaku-yen kitte o . . . mai kudasai
What's the postage for a letter to the U.S.?	アメリカ向けの手紙はいくらですか。	amerika muke no tegami wa ikura desu ka
What's the postage for a postcard to Britain?	イギリス向けの葉書はいくらですか。	igirisu muke no hagaki wa ikura desu ka
When will this letter get there?	いつごろ着きますか。	itsu goro tsukimasu ka
Do all letters go airmail?	手紙は全て航空便ですか。	tegami wa subete kōkûbin desu ka
I want to send this parcel.	この小包を送りたいのですが。	kono kozutsumi o okuritai no desu ga
Do I need to fill in a customs declaration form?	税関申告用紙に記入しなければなりませんか。	zeikan-shinkoku-yōshi ni kinyû shinakereba narimasen ka
I want to register this letter.	この手紙を書留にして下さい。	kono tegami o kakidome ni shite kudasai

Where's the letter-box?	郵便箱はどこですか。	yūbinbako wa doko desu ka
I want to send this by . . .	これを…で送って下さい。	kore o . . . de okutte kudasai
airmail	航空便	kōkūbin
express (special delivery)	速達	sokutatsu
recorded delivery	配達証明付き	haitatsu-shōmei-tsuki
registered mail	書留	kakidome
Where's the poste restante (general delivery)?	局留め郵便の窓口はどこですか。	kyokudome yūbin no madoguchi wa doko desu ka
Is there any mail for me? My name is . .	私宛に郵便が来ていますか。私の名前は…です。	watashi ate ni yūbin ga kite imasu ka watashi no namae wa . . . desu
Here's my passport.	これが私のパスポートです。	kore ga watashi no pasupōto desu

切手	STAMPS
小包	PARCELS
為替	MONEY ORDERS

Cables (telegrams)

Where's the nearest cable office?	最寄りの電報局はどこですか。	moyori no denpōkyoku wa doko desu ka
I want to send a cable (telegram). May I have a form, please?	電報を打ちたいのですが。用紙を頂けますか。	denpō o uchitai no desu ga yōshi o itadakemasu ka
How much is it per word?	一語に付きいくらですか。	ichigo ni tsuki ikura desu ka
How long will a cable to Boston take?	ボストンまで電報でどの位時間が掛かりますか。	bosuton made denpō de dono kurai jikan ga kakarimasu ka
Send it collect.	料金先方払いで送って下さい。	ryōkin-senpōbarai de okutte kudasai

Telephoning

There are many public telephone booths in the streets. If you can't find one, however, you can always try a tea-room or a bar or a railway station. Insert a 10-yen coin for all calls within the town limits. If there's no reply, the money is automatically refunded. Remember that in Tokyo you can't telephone for longer than three minutes, and that your call will automatically be cut after that time.

Dialling, which is on an inter-city basis for the larger towns, is straightforward. At the post office the operator will make the connection for you and charge you afterwards. Rates are cheaper after 8 p.m.

General

Where's the telephone?	電話はどこにありますか。	denwa wa doko ni arimasu ka
Where's the nearest telephone booth?	最寄りの公衆電話はどこにありますか。	moyori no kōshūdenwa wa doko ni arimasu ka
May I use your phone?	電話を貸して頂けますか。	denwa o kashite itadake-masu ka
Have you a telephone directory for Tokyo?	東京の電話帳をお持ちでしょうか。	tōkyō no denwachō o o-mochi deshō ka
Can you help me get this number?	この番号に電話したいのですけれど掛けて頂けませんか。	kono bangō ni denwa shitai no desu keredo kakete itadakemasen ka

Operator

Do you speak English?	英語を話しますか。	eigo o hanashi masu ka
Good morning. I want Tokyo 123–4567.	お早よう。東京123–4567番につないで下さい。	ohayō. tōkyō ichi-nii-san no yon-go-roku-shichi ban ni tsunaide kudasai
Can I dial direct?	ダイヤル直通ですか。	daiyaru-chokutsū desu ka

I want to place a person-to-person call.	パーソナルコールをお願いします。	pāsonaru kōru o o-negai shimasu
I want to reverse the charges (call collect).	料金先方払いにして下さい。	ryōkin-senpōbarai ni shite kudasai
Will you tell me the cost of the call afterwards?	料金を後で教えて下さい	ryōkin o atode oshiete kudasi

Speaking

I want to speak to . . .	…とお話ししたいのですが。	. . . to ohanashi shitai no desu ga
Would you put me through to . . . ?	…をお願いします。	. . . o o-negai shimasu
I want extension . . .	内線…をお願いします。	naisen . . . o o-negai shimasu
Is that . . . ?	…ですか。	. . . desu ka
Hello. This is . . .	もしもし…です。	moshi-moshi . . . desu

Bad luck

Would you try again later, please?	後でもう一回掛けて下さい。	atode mō ikkai kakete kudasai
Operator, you gave me the wrong number.	交換手さん，違う番号でした。	kōkanshu san chigau bangō deshita

Not there

When will he/she be back?	いつお帰りになりますか。	itsu okaeri ni narimasu ka
Will you tell him/her I called? My name is . . .	私から電話があったと伝えて頂けませんか。私は…と申します。	watashikara denwa ga attato tsutaete itadakemasen ka. watashi wa . . . to mōshimasu

Vould you ask her to all me?	私に電話するように伝えて頂けませんか。	watashi ni denwa suru yō ni tsutaete itadakemasen ka
Vould you take a nessage, please?	伝言を控えて頂けませんか。	dengon o hikaete itadakemasen ka

Charges

Vhat was the cost of hat call?	あの電話代はいくらでしたか。	ano denwadai wa ikura deshita ka
want to pay for the all.	電話代を払いたいのですが。	denwadai o haraitai no desu ga

Possible answers

貴方にお電話です。	There's a telephone call for you.
貴方にお電話です。	You're wanted on the telephone.
何番にお掛けになりましたか。	What number are you calling?
ふさがっています。	The line's engaged.
返事がありません。	There's no answer.
貴方の番号は間違っていますよ。	You've got the wrong number.
電話が故障です。	The phone is out of order.
彼は今外出中です。	He's out at the moment.

The car

We'll begin this section by considering your possible needs at filling station. Most filling stations don't handle major repairs but apart from provisioning you with fuel, they may be helpful i solving all kinds of minor problems.

Where's the nearest filling (service) station?	最寄りのガソリンスタンドはどこですか。	moyori no gasorin sutando wa doko desu ka
I want . . . litres, please.	…リットル入れて下さい。	. . . rittoru irete kudasai
I want 15 litres of standard.	スタンダードを15リットル入れて下さい。	sutandādo o jūgo rittoru irete kudasai
I want 25 litres of super.	スーパーを25リットル入れ下さい。	sūpā o ni-jū-go rittoru irete kudasai
Give me 2,000 yen worth of	…を2000円分入れて下さい。	. . . o nisen yen bun irete kudasai
Fill her up, please.	満タンにして下さい。	mantan ni shite kudasai
Check the oil and water, please.	オイルと水を調べて下さい。	oiru to mizu o shirabete kudasai
Give me . . . litres of oil.	オイルを…リットル下さい。	oiru o . . . rittoru kudasai
Top (fill) up the battery with distilled water.	バッテリの水を入れて下さい。	batterī no mizu o irete kudasa
Check the brake fluid.	ブレーキオイルを調べて下さい。	burēki oiru o shirabete kudasai

Fluid measures

litres	imp. gal.	U.S. gal.	litres	imp. gal.	U.S. gal.
5	1.1	1.3	30	6.6	7.8
10	2.2	2.6	35	7.7	9.1
15	3.3	3.9	40	8.8	10.4
20	4.4	5.2	45	9.9	11.7
25	5.5	6.5	50	11.0	13.0

FOR NUMBERS, see page 175

Tire pressure			
lb./sq. in.	kg/cm²	lb./sq. in	kg/cm²
10	0.7	26	1.8
12	0.8	27	1.9
15	1.1	28	2.0
18	1.3	30	2.1
20	1.4	33	2.3
21	1.5	36	2.5
23	1.6	38	2.7
24	1.7	40	2.8

Would you check the tires?	タイヤを調べて下さい。	taiya o shirabete kudasai
The pressure should be 1.6 front, 1.8 rear.	圧力は前が1.6で後は1.8ないといけません。	atsuryoku wa mae ga i-tten roku de ushiro wa i-tten hachi nai to ikemasen
Check the spare tire too, please.	スペアタイアも調べて下さい。	supeyā taiya mo shirabete kudasai
Can you mend this puncture (fix this flat)?	パンクを修理して下さい。	panku o shūri shite kudasai
Would you change this tire, please?	このタイヤを取り換えて下さい。	kono taiya o torikaete kudasai
Would you clean the windscreen (windshield)?	フロントガラスをふいて下さい。	furonto garasu o fuite kudasai
Have you a road map of this district?	この地方の道路地図をお持ちですか。	kono chihō no dōro-chizu o omochi desu ka
Where are the toilets?	手洗はどこですか。	te-arai wa doko desu ka

Asking the way—Street directions

Excuse me.	すみませんが。	sumimasen ga
Can you tell me the way to . . . ?	…へ行く道を教えて頂けませんか。	. . . e iku michi o oshiete itadakemasen ka
How do I get to . . . ?	…へはどう行けばいいでしょうか。	. . . e wa dō ikeba ii deshō ka

Where does this road lead to?	この道はどこに行く道ですか。	kono michi wa doko ni iku michi desu ka
Can you show me on this map where I am?	この地図で私がどこに居るか教えて下さい。	kono chizu de watashi ga doko ni iruka oshiete kudasa[i]
How far is it to . . . from here?	ここから…までどの位離れていますか。	kokokara . . . made dono kurai hanarete imasu ka

Miles into kilometres

1 mile = 1.609 kilometres (km)

miles	10	20	30	40	50	60	70	80	90	100
km	16	32	48	64	80	97	113	129	145	161

Kilometres into miles

1 kilometre (km) = 0.62 miles

km	10	20	30	40	50	60	70	80	90	100	110	120	130
miles	6	12	19	25	31	37	44	50	56	62	68	75	81

Possible answers

道を間違っていますよ。	You're on the wrong road.
真っすぐにいらっしゃい。	Go straight ahead.
この道を行って左側(右側)です。	It's down there on the left (right).
その方向です。	Go that way.
最初の(二番目)の四つ角までいらっしゃい。	Go to the first (second) crossroad.
信号の所で左に(右に)曲がりなさい。	Turn left (right) at the traffic lights.

the rest of this section, we'll be more closely concerned with e car itself. We've divided it into two parts:

rt A contains general advice on motoring in Japan. It's es- ntially for reference and therefore to be browsed over, pre- ably in advance.

rt B is concerned with the practical details of accidents and eakdown. It includes a list of car parts and a list of things that ay go wrong with them. All you have to do is to show the lists the garage mechanic and get him to point to the items required.

art A

ustoms—Documentation

inging private cars into Japan isn't so simple as in other coun- es and involves a considerable amount of red tape. You're erefore advised to ask the Japanese embassy or consulate your country for a copy of their leaflet "Customs Hints for inging Your Automobile to Japan" for full details.

u'll also require the following documents:

passport
international insurance certificate (green card)
international driving licence

e nationality plate or sticker must be on the car. A red angle—for display on the road in case of accidents—is a very portant accessory, and parking lights are advisable.

Here's my . . .	これが私の…です。	kore ga watashi no . . . . desu
driving licence	運転免許証	unten-menkyoshō
green card	グリーンカード	gurīnkādo
passport	パスポート	pasupōto
I haven't anything to declare.	何も申告する物はありません。	nani mo shinkoku suru mo wa arimasen
I have . . .	…持っています。	. . . motte imasu
a carton of cigarettes	タバコを一カートン	tabako o ichi-kāton
a bottle of whisky	ウィスキーを一本	uisukī o ippon
a bottle of wine	ぶどう酒を一本	budōshu o ippon
We're staying for . . .	…滞在するつもりです。	. . . . taizaisuru tsumori d
a week	一週間	isshū kan
two weeks	二週間	ni-shū kan
a month	一ヶ月	ikkagetsu

Roads

The road classification and map references in Japan are as follow

Kōsokudoro (motorway), a toll is charged according to the distan to be travelled and the size of the car.

No. 5, etc.—first-class main road.

Excellent bilingual road maps can be obtained from the Jap. Travel Bureau.

In Japan, you drive on the left hand side of the road and overtake on the right.

Driving around on your own in Japan cannot, in fact, be recommended, except on newly-built superhighways. Driving on the left may not be too hazardous for Americans in Great Britain, but when driving in Japan even the British themselves will probably not be at ease. Roads are often less than 15 feet wide and bumpy.

In many towns and cities, buildings encroach on roadsides without sidewalks, leaving pedestrians no alternative but to wind their way in and out of the heavy traffic. Often electricity poles are planted on roadsides. This may present a driving problem in narrower streets. There are also many railway level crossings. All things considered, it may be wiser to get a Japanese chauffeur who will be used to this state of affairs.

Parking

Use your common sense when parking. The police are normally lenient with foreign tourists, but don't push your luck too far. Obey the parking regulations indicated by signs or red lines painted on the kerb (curb).

Excuse me. May I park here?	ちょっとお尋ねします。ここに駐車出来ますか。	chotto o-tazune shimasu. koko ni chūsha dekimasu ka
How long may I park here?	ここに何時間位駐車出来ますか。	koko ni nan jikan gurai chūsha dekimasu ka
What's the charge for parking here?	ここの駐車料金はいくらですか。	koko no chūsha-ryōkin wa ikura desu ka
Must I leave my lights on?	ライトを付けたままにして置かないといけませんか。	raito o tsuketa mama ni shite okanai to ikemasen ka

Japanese road signs

Here are some of the main signs and notices you are likely to encounter when driving in Japan:

安全運転	Drive safely
一方通行	One-way traffic
追越し禁止	No overtaking (passing)
横断歩道	Pedestrian crossing
危険	Danger
カーブ危険	Dangerous bend (curve)
左折可	Left turn allowed at any time
砂利道	Loose gravel
自転車専用	Bicycles only
重量制限	Weight limit
車両通行止め	No vehicles
徐行	Slow
信号機あり	Traffic lights ahead
スピード落せ	Reduce speed
前方優先道路	Main road (thoroughfare) ahead
高さ制限	Height limit
注意	Caution
駐車禁止	No parking
駐停車禁止	No parking or stopping
転回禁止	No U turn
道路工事中	Roadworks in progress
止まれ	Stop
二方向交通	Oncoming traffic
バス停留所	Bus stop
踏切あり	Level (railroad) crossing
歩行者注意	Caution: pedestrians
歩行者専用	Pedestrians only
本線	Through traffic
まわり道	Diversion (detour)
優先	Priority (right of way)
行き止まり	Cul-de-sac (dead-end road)
路肩弱し	Soft shoulder
路面凹凸あり	Bad road surface

'art B

\ccidents

his section is confined to immediate aid. The legal problems of :sponsibility and settlement can be taken care of at a later stage. 'our first concern will be for the injured.

; anyone hurt?	怪我人がいますか。	keganin ga imasu ka
on't move.	動かないで下さい。	ugokanai de kudasai
's all right. Don't vorry.	大丈夫です。心配しないで下さい。	daijōbu desu. shinpai shinai de kudasai
/here's the nearest elephone?	最寄りの電話はどこですか。	moyori no denwa wa doko desu ka
1ay I use your elephone?	電話を貸して頂けますか。	denwa o kashite itadakemasu ka
nere's been an ccident.	事故がありました。	jiko ga arimashita
all a doctor ambulance) quickly.	お医者さん(救急車)をすぐに呼んで下さい。	o-isha san (kyūkyūsha) o suguni yonde kudasai
here are people ijured.	怪我人がいます。	keganin ga imasu
elp me get them ut of the car.	車から出すのを手伝って下さい。	kuruma kara dasu no o tetsudatte kudasai

'olice—Exchange of information

'lease call the police.	警察を呼んで下さい。	keisatsu o yonde kudasai
here's been an ccident.	事故がありました。	jiko ga arimashita
:'s about 2 km 'om . . .	現場は…から2キロ程の所です。	genba wa . . . kara ni kiro hodo no tokoro desu
'm on the Tokyo-'okohama road, 13 m from Tokyo.	東京横浜間にいます。東京から13キロの所です。	tōkyō yokohama kan ni imasu. tōkyō kara jūsan kiro no tokoro desu.

Here's my name and address.	これが私の名前と住所です。	kore ga watashi no namae to jūsho desu
Would you mind acting as a witness?	証人になって頂けますか。	shōnin ni natte itadakemas ka
I'd like an interpreter.	通訳の人に来てもらいたいのですが。	tsūyaku no hito ni kite moraitai no desu ga

Remember to put out a red triangle warning if the car is out c action or impeding traffic.

Breakdown

. . . and that's what we'll do with this section: break it down int four phases.

1. **On the road**
   You ask where the nearest garage is.
2. **At the garage**
   You tell the mechanic what's wrong.
3. **Finding the trouble**
   He tells you what he thinks is wrong.
4. **Getting it fixed**
   You tell him to fix it and, once that is done, settle the accou (or argue about it).

Phase 1—On the road

Where's the nearest garage?	最寄りのガレージはどこですか。	moyori no garēji wa doko desu ka
Excuse me. My car has broken down. May I use your phone?	恐れ入ります。車が故障してしまいました。電話を貸して頂けませんか。	osoreirimasu. kuruma ga koshō shite shimaimashita. denwa o kashite itadake-masen ka

What's the telephone number of the nearest garage?	最寄りのガレージの電話番号は何番ですか。	moyori no garēji no denwabangō wa nanban desu ka
I've had a breakdown at . . .	…で車が故障しました。	. . . de kuruma ga koshō shimashita
We're on the Tokyo-Yokohama motorway (expressway), about 13 km from Tokyo.	東京横浜高速道路の東京から13キロの所です。	tōkyō-yokohama kōsokudōro no tōkyō kara jūsan kiro no tokoro desu
Can you send a mechanic?	修理する人をよこして下さい。	shūri suru hito o yokoshite kudasai
Can you send a truck to tow my car?	レッカーをよこして下さい。	rekkā o yokoshite kudasai
How long will you be?	どの位時間が掛かりますか。	dono kurai jikan ga kakarimasu ka

Phase 2—At the garage

Can you help me?	お願い出来ますか。	o-negai dekimasu ka
Can you repair my car?	車を修理して頂けますか。	kuruma o shūri shite itadakemasu ka
I don't know what's wrong with it.	どこが悪いか分かりません。	doko ga warui ka wakari-masen
I think there's some-thing wrong with the . . .	…が悪いと思います。	. . . ga warui to omoimasu
battery	バッテリ	batteri
brakes	ブレーキ	burēki
bulbs	ライト	raito
clutch	クラッチ	kuratchi
cooling system	冷却装置	reikyakusōchi
contact	コンタクト	kontakuto
dimmers	ディマー	dimā
dynamo	ダイナモ	dainamo

electrical system	電気装置	denkisōchi
engine	エンジン	enjin
gears	ギャ	giya
generator	ダイナモ	dainamo
handbrake	ハンドブレーキ	hando burēki
headlight	ヘッドライト	heddoraito
horn	クラクション	kurakushon
ignition system	点火装置	tenkasōchi
indicator	方向指示器	hōkōshijiki
lights	ライト	raito
brake light	ブレーキランプ	burēkiranpu
reversing (back-up) light	バックライト	bakku raito
tail lights	テールライト	tēruraito
lubrication system	潤滑油装置	jyunkatsuyusōchi
pedal	ペダル	pedaru
reflectors	リフレクター	rifurekutā
sparking plugs	点火プラグ	tenkapuragu
starting motor	スターター	sutātā
steering	ステアリング	sutearingu
suspension	サスペンション	sasupenshon
transmission	トランスミッション	toransumisshon
wheels	車輪	sharin
wipers	ワイパー	waipā

RIGHT	LEFT	FRONT	BACK
右 (migi)	左 (hidari)	前 (mae)	後 (ushiro)

It's . . .	…	
bad	悪いです	warui desu
blowing	漏れています	morete imasu
blown	熔解しています	yōkaishite imasu
broken	こわれています	kowarete imasu
burnt	焼けています	yakete imasu
cracked	ひびが入っています	hibi ga haitte imasu
defective	不良です	furyō desu
disconnected	はずれています	hazurete imasu
dry	かわいています	kawaite imasu
frozen	氷っています	kōtte imasu

CAR—REPAIRS

nmed	動きません	ugokimasen
ocking	ノッキングしています	nokkingushite imasu
king	漏れています	morete imasu
se	ゆるんでいます	yurunde imasu
sfiring	着火しません	chakka shimasen
'sy	音がします	oto ga shimasu
t working	動きません	ugokimasen
erheating	オーバーヒートしています	ōbāhīto shite imasu
ort-circuiting	ショートしています	shōto shite imasu
ck	ゆるんでいます	yurunde imasu
oping	すべっています	subette imasu
ck	付着しています	fuchaku shite imasu
rating	震動しています	shindō shite imasu
ak	弱いです	yowai desu
orn	すり減っています	surihette imasu
e car won't start.	エンジンが掛かりません。	enjin ga kakarimasen
s locked and the ys are inside.	キーを中に置いたままドアをロックしてしまいました。	kī o naka ni oitamama doa o rokku shite shimaimashita
e fan-belt is too ck.	ファンベルトがゆるんでいます。	fuanberuto ga yurunde imasu
e radiator is king.	ラジエーターが漏れています。	rajiētā ga morete imasu
e idling needs justing.	キャブレータのアイドリングの調整が必要です。	kyaburetā no aidoringu no chōsei ga hitsuyō desu
e clutch engages o quickly.	クラッチがすぐつながってしまいます。	kuratchi ga sugu tsunagatte shimaimasu
e steering wheel is rating.	ハンドルが震動します。	handoru ga shindō shimasu
e wipers are nearing.	ワイパーがよごれています。	waipā ga yogorete imasu
e pedal needs justing.	ペダルの調整が必要です。	pedaru no chōsei ga hitsuyō desu

ow that you've explained what's wrong, you'll want to know ow long it'll take to repair it and arrange yourself accordingly.

How long will it take to repair?	修理にどの位時間が掛かりますか。	shūri ni dono kurai jikan ga kakarimasu ka
Suppose I come back in half an hour (tomorrow)?	30分以内に(明日)又もどって来ましょう。	sanji-ppun inai ni (asu) mata modotte kimasho
Can you give me a lift into town?	市内まで車で連れて行って頂けますか。	shinai made kuruma de tsurete itte itadakemasu k
Is there a place to stay nearby?	この近くにどこか一泊できる所がありますか。	kono chikaku ni dokoka ippaku dekiru tokoro ga arimasu ka
May I use your phone?	電話を貸して頂けますか。	denwa o kashite itadakemasu ka

Phase 3—Finding the trouble

If you don't know what's wrong with the car, it's up to the m chanic to find the trouble. You can ask him what has to be r paired by handing him the book and pointing to the Japane text below.

次のリストを御覧になって故障個所を教えて下さい。尚，故障の態については次頁のリストを御覧になって下さい。*

イグニッションコイル	ignition coil
インジェクションポンプ	injection pump
エアサスペンション	pneumatic suspension
エアフィルター	air filter
エンジン	engine
オイルフィルター	oil filter
オートマティックトランスミッション	automatic transmission
カム軸	camshaft
ガソリンフィルター	petrol filter

* Please look at the following alphabetical list and point to the defective item. If your custo wants to know what is wrong with it, pick the applicable term from the next list (brok short-circuited, etc.).

ガソリンポンプ	petrol pump
キャブレター	carburettor
ギヤ	gear
ギヤボックス	gearbox
クラッチ	clutch
クラッチペダル	clutch pedal
クラッチプレート	clutch plate
クランクケース	crankcase
クランク軸	crankshaft
グリース	grease
ケーブル	cable
コネクション	connection
コンタクトポイント	points
サーモスタット	thermostat
サスペンション	suspension
軸受	bearing
シリンダー	cylinder
シリンダーパッキング	cylinder head gasket
シリンダーブロック	block
シリンダーヘッド	cylinder head
車輪	wheels
シュー	shoes
主軸受	main bearings
ジョイント	joint
ショックアブソーバー	shock-absorber
スターター	starting motor
スタビライザー	stabilizer
スティアリング	steering
スティアリングボックス	steering box
ステム	stems
スプリング	springs
接点	contact
タペット	tappets
ダイナモ	dynamo (generator)
ディストリビューター	distributor
ディストリビューターリード	distributor leads
点火プラグ	sparking plugs
点火プラグリード	sparking plug leads
電気装置	electrical system
トランスミッション	transmission
歯	teeth
ハンドル軸	steering column
バッテリ	battery

バッテリ液	battery liquid
バッテリセル	battery cells
バルブ	valve
バルブスプリング	valve spring
ピストン	piston
ピストンリング	piston rings
フィルター	filter
ブラシ	brushes
ブレーキ	brake
ブレーキドラム	brake drum
プレッシャースプリング	pressure-springs
フロート	float
ファン	fan
ファンベルト	fan-belt
ポンプ	pump
膜	diaphragm
水ポンプ	water pump
ユニバーサルジョイント	universal joint
冷却装置	cooling system
ラジエーター	radiator
ライニング	lining
ラックアンドピニオン	rack and pinion
リング	rings

次のリストに故障の状態及び修理法が列記してあります。*

遊び	play
動かない	jammed
オーバーヒートしている	overheating
かわいている	dry
研摩する	to grind in
交換する	to change
交換する	to replace
こわれている	broken
こおりついている	frozen
充電する	to charge
締める	to tighten

*The following list contains words about what's wrong or what may have to be done with the car.

ョートしている	short-circuit
動している	vibrating
リップしている	slipping
り減っている	worn
除する	to clean
い	high
火しない	misfiring
整する	to adjust
ッキングしている	knocking
ずれている	disconnected
い	quick
ンク	puncture
ランスする	to balance
びが入っている	cracked
蝕している	corroded
い	low
着している	stuck
良である	defective
解する	to strip down
がっている	warped
い	short
れている	blowing
れている	leaking
けている	burnt
るめる	to loosen
るんでいる	loose
解している	blown
ごれている	dirty
るんでいる	slack
い	weak
イニングを取り替える	to reline

hase 4—Getting it fixed

ave you found the ouble?	悪い個所が分かりましたか。	warui kasho ga wakarimashita ka

ow that you know what's wrong, or at least have some idea, u may want to find out. . .

Is that serious?	ひどいですか。	hidoi desu ka
Can you fix it?	修理出来ますか。	shūri dekimasu ka
Can you do it now?	今出来ますか。	ima dekimasu ka
What's it going to cost?	いくら掛かるでしょうか。	ikura kakaru deshō ka
Have you the necessary spare parts?	必要な部品がありますか。	hitsuyō na buhin ga arima ka

What if he says "no"?

Why can't you do it?	どうして出来ないのですか。	dōshite dekinai no desu k
Is it essential to have that part?	その部品がないと全然だめですか。	sono buhin ga naito zenze dame desu ka
How long is it going to take to get the spare parts?	部品を手に入れるにはどの位掛かりますか。	buhin o teniireru ni wa dono kurai kakarimasu ka
Where's the nearest garage that can repair it?	それを修理出来る最寄りのガレージはどこにありますか。	sore o shūri dekiru moyori garēji wa doko ni arimasu
Well, can you fix it so that I can get as far as . . . ?	では…まで行けるように何んとかしてもらえますか。	dewa . . . made ikeru yō nantoka shite moraemasu

If you're really stuck, ask if you can leave the car at the garag Contact an automobile association. . .or hire another car.

Settling the bill

Is everything fixed?	全部修理出来ましたか。	zenbu shūri dekimashita k
How much do I owe you?	おいくらですか。	o-ikura desu ka

The garage then presents you with a bill. If you're satisfied . . .

Will you take a traveller's cheque (check)?	トラベラーチェックでいいですか。	toraberā cheku de ii desu ka
Thank you very much for your help.	どうもありがとう助かりました。	dōmo arigatō tasukarimashita
This is for you.	これは心づけです。	kore wa kokorozuke desu

But you may feel that the workmanship is sloppy or that you're paying for work not done. Get the bill itemized. If necessary, get it translated before you pay.

I'd like to check the bill first. Will you itemize the work done?	支払う前に請求書を調べて見たいのですが，修理の明細書を頂けますか。	shiharau maeni seikyūsho o shirabete mitai no desu ga shūri no meisaisho o itadakemasu ka

If the garage still won't back down—and you're sure you're right—get the help of a third party.

Some Japanese road signs

Road closed

No vehicles

No entry (one way)

No automobiles

No right turn

No U turn

No overtaking (passing)

No vehicles carrying explosive or inflammable materials

Minimum speed

Speed limit

No stopping

No parking

Stop

Slow down

Closed to pedestrians

Crossing by pedestrians prohibited

Caution

Uneven road

Level crossing (railroad crossing)

Danger from crosswinds

Motor vehicles only

Sound horn

Go straight

End of restriction

One way

Priority road (thoroughfare)

Bus lane

Emergency parking zone

Driving on tramway permitted

Stopping permitted

Parking

Safety zone

Doctor

Frankly, how much use is a phrase book going to be to you in the case of serious injury or illness? The only phrase you need in such an emergency is. . .

Get a doctor—quick!	早く医者を！	hayaku isha o

But there are minor aches and pains, ailments and irritations that can upset the best planned trip. Here we can help you—and, perhaps, the doctor.

Some doctors will speak English well; others will know enough for your needs. But suppose there is something the doctor cannot explain because of language difficulties? We've thought of that.

As you will see, this section has been arranged to enable you and the doctor to communicate. From page 165 to 171, you will find your side of the dialogue on the upper half of each page; the doctor's is on the lower half.

The whole section has been divided into three parts: illness, wounds, nervous tension. Page 171 is concerned with prescriptions and fees.

General

I need a doctor—quickly.	医者を呼んで下さい。早く。	isha o yonde kudasai. hayaku
Can you get me a doctor?	医者を呼んで下さいますか。	isha o yonde kudasaimasu ka
Is there a doctor in the hotel?	ホテルに医者がいますか。	hoteru ni isha ga imasu ka
Please telephone for a doctor immediately.	すぐに電話で医者を呼んで下さい。	suguni denwa de isha o yonde kudasai
Where's a doctor who speaks English?	どこに行けば英語を話す医者がいますか。	doko ni ikeba eigo o hanasu isha ga imasu ka

Is there an English/ American hospital in town?	この町にイギリス／アメリカの病院がありますか。	kono machi ni igirisu/ amerika no byōin ga arimasu ka
Where's the doctor's office (surgery)?	医者はどこですか。	isha wa doko desu ka
What are the office (surgery) hours?	診察時間は何時から何時までですか。	shinsatsu-jikan wa nanji kara nanji made desu ka
Could the doctor come and see me here?	医者にここに来て見てもらえますか。	isha ni koko ni kite mite moraemasu ka
What time can the doctor come?	医者は何時に来てくれますか。	isha wa nanji ni kite kuremasu ka

Symptoms

Use this section to tell the doctor what is wrong. Basically, what he'll require to know is:

What? (ache, pain, bruise, etc.)
Where? (arm, stomach, etc.)
How long? (have you had the trouble)

Before you visit the doctor find out the answers to these questions by glancing through the pages that follow. In this way you'll save time.

Parts of the body

ankle	足首	ashikubi
appendix	盲腸	mōchō
arm	腕	ude
artery	動脈	dōmyaku
back	背中	senaka
bladder	膀胱	bōkō
blood	血	chi
bone	骨	hone
bowels	腸	chō
breast	乳房	chibusa

chest	胸	mune
collar-bone	鎖骨	sakotsu
ear	耳	mimi
elbow	肘	hiji
eye	目	me
face	顔	kao
finger	指	yubi
foot	足	ashi
gland	腺	sen
hand	手	te
head	頭	atama
heart	心臓	shinzō
heel	踵	kakato
hip	尻	shiri
intestines	腸	chō
jaw	顎	ago
joint	関節	kansetsu
kidney	腎臓	jinzō
knee	膝	hiza
leg	脚	ashi
liver	肝臓	kanzō
lung	肺	hai
mouth	口	kuchi
muscle	筋肉	kinniku
neck	首	kubi
nerve	神経	shinkei
nervous system	神経系統	shinkei keito
nose	鼻	hana
rib	肋骨	rokkotsu
shoulder	肩	kata
skin	皮膚	hifu
spine	背骨	sebone
stomach	胃	i
tendon	腱	ken
thigh	腿	momo
throat	喉	nodo
thumb	親指	oyayubi
toe	足指	ashinoyubi
tongue	舌	shita
tonsils	扁桃腺	hentōsen
urine	尿	nyō
vein	静脈	jōmyaku
wrist	手首	tekubi

ATIENT

art 1—Illness

m not feeling well.	気分がすぐれません。	kibun ga suguremasen
m ill.	具合が悪いのですが。	guai ga warui no desu ga
ve got a pain here.	ここが痛みます。	koko ga itamimasu
lis/Her . . . hurts.	…が痛いんです。	. . . ga itain desu
've got a . . .	…が痛みます。	. . . ga itami masu
eadache/backache/ sore throat	頭／背中／のど	atama/senaka/nodo
'm constipated.	便秘してます。	benpi shitemasu
've been vomiting.	戻しました。	modoshimashita

OCTOR

の1—症状

うなすったのですか。	What's the trouble?
こが痛みますか。	Where does it hurt?
み出してからどの位になりますか。	How long have you had this pain?
んな状態がどの位続いていますか。	How long have you been feeling like this?
をまくって下さい。	Roll up your sleeve.
半身服を脱いで下さい。	Please undress (down to the waist).
ボンとパンツを脱いで下さい。	Please remove your trousers and underpants.

PATIENT

I feel . . .	私は…	watashi wa . . .
ill/sick	気分が悪いです	kibun ga warui desu
faint/dizzy	ふらふらします／めまいがします	furafura shimasu/memai ga shimasu
nauseous/shivery	吐気がします／寒気がします	hakike ga shimasu/samuke ga shimasu
I/He/She's got (a/an) . . .	私は／彼は／彼女は…	watashi wa/kare wa/kanojo wa . . .
abcess	腫物ができました	haremono ga dekimashita
asthma	喘息です	zensoku desu
chill	悪寒を感じます	okan o kanjimasu
cold	風邪をひきました	kaze o hikimashita
constipation	便秘しています	benpi shite imasu
convulsions	けいれんしました	keiren shimashita
cramps	けいれんしました	keiren shimashita
diarrhoea	下痢しています	geri shite imasu
fever	熱があります	netsu ga arimasu
haemorrhoids	痔疾です	jishitsu desu

DOCTOR

ここに横になって下さい。	Please lie down over here.
口を開けて下さい。	Open your mouth.
深呼吸をして下さい。	Breathe deeply.
咳をして下さい。	Cough, please.
体温を計って見ましょう。	I'll take your temperature.
血圧を計って見ましょう。	I'm going to take your blood pressure.
これは始めてですか。	Is this the first time you've had this?
注射をしましょう。	I'll give you an injection.
尿を／便を検査しましょう。	I want a specimen of your urine/stools.

PATIENT

hernia	ヘルニヤに罹っています	heruniya ni kakatte imasu
indigestion	消化不良を起しています	shōkafuryō o okoshite imasu
inflammation of . . .	…が炎症を起しています	. . . ga enshō o okoshite imasu
influenza	流感に罹っています	ryūkan ni kakatte imasu
morning sickness	つわりです	tsuwari desu
stiff neck	首が廻らない	kubi ga mawara nai
rheumatism	リューマチです	ryumachi desu
sunburn	日焼けです	hiyake desu
sunstroke	日射病です	nisshabyō desu
tonsillitis	扁桃腺炎です	hentosenen desu
ulcer	潰瘍です	kaiyō desu
It's nothing serious, I hope?	大した事はないでしょうね。	taishita koto wa nai deshō ne
I'd like you to prescribe me some medicine.	何か薬を処方して下さい。	nanika kusuri o shohō shite kudasai

DOCTOR

何も心配する事はありません。	It's nothing to worry about.
…日間の安静が必要です。	You must stay in bed for . . . days.
貴方は…	You've got . . .
風邪をひいていますね/関節炎ですね/肺炎ですね/流感ですね/食中毒ですね/…の炎症ですね	a cold/arthritis/pneumonia/influenza/food poisoning/an inflammation of . . .
煙草の吸い過ぎです/お酒の飲み過ぎです。	You're smoking/drinking too much.
過労です。休養が必要です。	You're over-tired. You need a rest.
専門医に見てもらいなさい。	I want you to see a specialist.
検査のため病院に行って下さい。	I want you to go to the hospital for a general check-up.
抗生物質を処方しましょう。	I'll prescribe an antibiotic.

PATIENT

I'm a diabetic.	私は糖尿病に罹っています。	watashi wa tōnyōbyō ni kakatte imasu
I've a cardiac condition.	心臓病の気があります。	shinzōbyō no ke ga arimasu
I've had a heart attack in . . .	…に心臓発作がありました。	. . . ni shinzō-hossa ga arimashita
I'm allergic to . . .	…に対してアレルギーです。	. . . ni taishite arerugī desu
This is my usual medicine.	いつも飲んでいる薬はこれです。	itsumo nonde iru kusuri wa kore desu
I need this medicine.	この薬が欲しいのですが	kono kusuri ga hoshii no desu ga
I'm expecting a baby.	妊娠しています。	ninshin shite imasu
Can I travel?	旅行しても構いませんか。	ryokō shite mo kamaimasen ka

DOCTOR

インシュリンの一回の服用量はどの位ですか。	What dose of insulin are you taking?
注射ですか。それとも飲み薬ですか。	Injection or oral?
どういう治療を受けていますか。	What treatment have you been having?
どんな薬を使っていますか。	What medicine have you been taking?
(軽い)心臓発作です。	You've had a (slight) heart attack.
…は日本では使っていません。これは類似の薬です。	We don't use . . . in Japan. This is very similar.
出産予定はいつですか。	When is the baby due?
…まで旅行はだめです。	You can't travel until . . .

PATIENT

Part 2—Wounds

Could you have a look at this . . . ?	この…を見て頂けますか。	kono . . . o mite itadakemasu ka
blister	水腫	mizubukure
boil	できもの	dekimono
bruise	打撲傷	dabokushō
burn	火傷	yakedo
cut	切り傷	kirikizu
graze	かすり傷	kasurikizu
insect bite	虫刺され	mushisasare
lump	瘤	kobu
rash	発疹	hasshin
sting	刺され傷	sasarekizu
swelling	腫物	haremono
wound	傷	kizu
I can't move my . . . . It hurts.	…が痛くて動かせません。	. . . ga itakute ugokase masen

---

DOCTOR

その2—傷の手当

化膿しています。(いません。)	It's (not) infected.
脱臼しています。	You've got a slipped disc.
レントゲンをとる必要があります。	I want you to have an X-ray.
…います。	It's . . .
折れて/挫いて 脱臼して/裂けて	broken/sprained dislocated/torn
筋肉を張り過ぎたようですね。	You've pulled a muscle.
抗生物質を上げましょう。 大した事はありません。	I'll give you an antiseptic. It's not serious.
…日たったらもう一度来て下さい。	I want you to come and see me in . . . days' time.

PATIENT

Part 3—Nervous tension

I'm in a nervous state.	神経過敏の状態です。	shinkeikabin no jōtai desu
I'm feeling depressed.	気がふさいでいます。	ki ga fusaide imasu
I want some sleeping pills.	睡眠薬が欲しいのですが。	suiminyaku ga hoshiino desu ga
I can't eat/sleep.	食が進みません。／眠れません。	shoku ga susumimasen/ nemuremasen
I'm having nightmares.	夢でうなされます。	yume de unasare masu
Can you prescribe a . . . ?	…を処方して頂けますか。	. . . o shohō shite itadake masu ka
sedative	鎮静剤	chinseizai
tranquilizer	トランキライザー	torankiraizā
anti-depressant	アンティーディプレサント	anti-depuresanto

DOCTOR

その3—神経過敏症

神経過敏症ですね。	You're suffering from nervous tension.
休養が必要です。	You need a rest.
どんな薬を使っていますか。	What pills have you been taking?
一日何錠ですか。	How many a day?
どの位こんな状態が続いていますか。	How long have you been feeling like this?
薬を処方して上げましょう。	I'll prescribe some pills.
鎮静剤を上げましょう。	I'll give you a sedative.

PATIENT

Prescriptions and dosage

What kind of medicine is this?	これはどんな薬ですか。	kore wa donna kusuri desu ka
How many times a day should I take it?	一日に何回飲まなければなりませんか。	ichinichi ni nankai noma-nakereba narimasen ka
Must I swallow them whole?	全部このまま飲み下さなければいけませんか。	zenbu konomama nomikudasa-nakereba ikemasen ka

Fee

How much do I owe you?	おいくらですか。	o-ikura desu ka
Do I pay you now or will you send me your bill?	今お払いしましょうか。それとも請求書を送って頂けますか。	ima o-harai shimashō ka. soretomo sēkyūsho o okutte itadakemasu ka
Thanks for your help, doctor.	どうも色々ありがとうございました。	dōmo iroiro arigatō gozaimashita

---

DOCTOR

薬の処方

この薬を…時間毎に薬さじ…杯飲んで下さい。	Take . . . teaspoons of this medicine every . . . hours.
これを…錠 コップ一杯の水で飲んで下さい。	Take . . . tablets with a glass of water.
一日に…回	. . . times a day
食事の前に	before each meal
食事の後に	after each meal
朝	in the mornings
夜	at night

治療費

千円です。	That's 1000 yen, please.
今払って下さい。	Please pay me now.
請求書は後でお送りします。	I'll send you a bill.

Dentist

Can you recommend a good dentist?	良い歯医者を紹介して頂けますか。	yoi haisha o shōkai shite itadakemasu ka
Can I make an (urgent) appointment to see Doctor . . . ?	(至急)…先生に見て頂きたいのですが。	(shikyū) . . . sensei ni mite itadakitai no desu ga
Can't you possibly make it earlier than that?	もっと早く出来ませんか。	motto hayaku dekimasen ka
I've a toothache.	歯が痛みます。	ha ga itamimasu
I've an abcess.	腫物が出来てます。	haremono ga dekite imasu
This tooth hurts.	この歯が痛みます。	kono ha ga itamimasu
at the top at the bottom in the front at the back	上です 下です 前です 奥です	ue desu shita desu mae desu oku desu
Can you fix it temporarily?	応急処置をして頂けますか。	ōkyūshochi o shite itadakemasu ka
I don't want it extracted (pulled).	抜かないで下さい。	nukanai de kudasai
I've lost a filling.	詰め物を無くしました。	tsumemono o nakushi mashita
The gum is very sore/ The gum is bleeding.	歯茎がとても痛みます／歯茎が出血しています。	haguki ga totemo itamimasu/haguki ga shukketsu shite imasu

Dentures

I've broken this denture.	入歯をこわしてしまいました。	ireba o kowashite shimaimashita
Can you repair this denture?	この入歯を直して頂けますか。	kono ireba o naoshite itadakemasu ka
When will it be ready?	いつ出来上りますか。	itsu dekiagarimasu ka

·ptician

ve broken my lasses.	眼鏡をこわしてしまいました。	megane o kowashite shimaimashita
an you repair them ɔr me?	直して頂けますか。	naoshite itadakemasu ka
/hen will they be ɜady?	いつ出来上りますか。	itsu dekiagarimasu ka
an you change the ·nses?	レンズを取り替えて頂けますか。	renzu o torikaete itadakemasu ka
want some contact ·nses.	コンタクトレンズが欲しいのですが。	kontakuto-renzu ga hoshii no desu ga
want tinted lenses.	色の付いたレンズが欲しいのですが。	iro no tsuita renzu ga hoshii no desu ga
d like to buy a pair f binoculars.	双眼鏡を一つ買いたいのですが。	sōgankyō o hitotsu kaitai no desu ga
·ow much do I owe ɔu?	おいくらですか。	o-ikura desu ka
·o I pay you now or vill you send me your ill?	今お払いしましょうか。それとも請求書を送って下さいますか。	ima o-harai shimashō ka. soretomo seikyūsho o okutte kudasaimasu ka.

ɔR NUMBERS, see page 175

Reference section

Where do you come from?

This page will help you to explain where you're from, wh
you've been or where you're going.

Africa	アフリカ	afurika
Asia	アジア	ajia
Australia	オーストラリア	ōsutoraria
Belgium	ベルギー	berugī
Burma	ビルマ	biruma
Canada	カナダ	kanada
China	中国	chūgoku
Denmark	デンマーク	denmāku
Europe	ヨーロッパ	yōroppa
Finland	フィンランド	finrando
France	フランス	furansu
Germany	ドイツ	doitsu
Great Britain	イギリス	igirisu
Holland	オランダ	oranda
India	インド	indo
Indonesia	インドネシア	indoneshia
Ireland	アイルランド	airurando
Italy	イタリー	itarī
Japan	日本	nippon
Korea	韓国	kankoku
Malaysia	マレーシア	marēshia
New Zealand	ニュージーランド	nyūjīrando
North America	北米	hokubē
Norway	ノルウエー	noruē
Philippines	フィリッピン	firippin
South Africa	南アフリカ	mimami afurika
South America	南米	nanbē
Sweden	スウェーデン	suēden
Switzerland	スイス	suisu
Taiwan	台湾	taiwan
Thailand	タイ国	taikoku
USA	アメリカ	amerika
USSR	ソ連	soren

Numbers

1	一	ichi
2	二	ni
3	三	san
4	四	shi (yon, yo)
5	五	go
6	六	roku
7	七	shichi (nana)
8	八	hachi
9	九	kyū (ku)
10	十	jū
11	十一	jū-ichi
12	十二	jū-ni
13	十三	jū-san
14	十四	jū-shi
15	十五	jū-go
16	十六	jū-roku
17	十七	jū-shichi
18	十八	jū-hachi
19	十九	jū-kyū (jūku)
20	二十	ni-jū
21	二十一	ni-jū-ichi
22	二十二	ni-jū-ni
23	二十三	ni-jū-san
24	二十四	ni-jū-shi
25	二十五	ni-jū-go
26	二十六	ni-jū-roku
27	二十七	ni-jū-shichi
28	二十八	ni-jū-hachi
29	二十九	ni-jū-kyū (ni-jū-ku)
30	三十	san-jū
31	三十一	san-jū-ichi
32	三十二	san-jū-ni
33	三十三	san-jū-san
40	四十	yon-jū
41	四十一	yon-jū-ichi
42	四十二	yon-jū-ni
43	四十三	yon-jū-san
50	五十	go-jū
51	五十一	go-jū-ichi
52	五十二	go-jū-ni
53	五十三	go-jū-san

60	六十	roku-jū
61	六十一	roku-jū-ichi
62	六十二	roku-jū-ni
70	七十	nana-jū
71	七十一	nana-jū-ichi
72	七十二	nana-jū-ni
80	八十	hachi-jū
81	八十一	hachi-jū-ichi
82	八十二	hachi-jū-ni
90	九十	kyū-jū
91	九十一	kyū-jū-ichi
92	九十二	kyū-jū-ni
100	百	hyaku
101	百一	hyaku-ichi
102	百二	hyaku-ni
110	百十	hyaku-jū
120	百二十	hyaku-ni-jū
130	百三十	hyaku-san-jū
140	百四十	hyaku-yon-jū
150	百五十	hyaku-go-jū
160	百六十	hyaku-roku-jū
170	百七十	hyaku-nana-jū
180	百八十	hyaku-hachi-jū
190	百九十	hyaku-kyū-jū
200	二百	ni-hyaku
300	三百	san-byaku
400	四百	yon-hyaku
500	五百	go-hyaku
600	六百	ro-ppyaku
700	七百	nana-hyaku
800	八百	ha-ppyaku
900	九百	kyū-hyaku
1000	千	sen
1100	千百	sen-hyaku
1200	千二百	sen-ni-hyaku
2000	二千	ni-sen
5000	五千	go-sen
10,000	一万	ichi-man
50,000	五万	go-man
100,000	十万	jū-man
1,000,000	百万	hyaku-man
1,000,000,000	十億	jū-oku

first	一番	ichiban
second	二番	niban
third	三番	sanban
fourth	四番	yonban (yoban)
fifth	五番	goban
sixth	六番	rokuban
seventh	七番	shichiban (nanaban)
eighth	八番	hachiban
ninth	九番	kyūban (kuban)
tenth	十番	jūban
once	一度	ichido
twice	二度	nido
three times	三度	sando
a half	半分	hanbun
half a . . .	…の半分	. . . no hanbun
half of . . .	…の半分	. . . no hanbun
half (adj.)	半分	hanbun
a quarter	四分の一	yonbun no ichi
one third	三分の一	sanbun no ichi
a pair of	一組の	hitokumi no
a dozen	一ダース	ichi-dāsu
1978	千九百七十八	sen-kyū-hyaku-nana-jū-hachi
1979	千九百七十九	sen-kyū-hyaku-nana-jū-kyū
1980	千九百八十	sen-kyū-hyaku-hachi-jū

Note: In Japanese, some cardinal numbers are pronounced in two or three different ways though they're written alike. **Shi, yon** or **yo** may be used for saying the number four, **shichi** or **nana** for seven and **ku** or **kyū** for nine. With rare exception any alternative pronunciation may be used in conversation.

We'd recommend, however, that you use **yon** for four, **nana** for seven and **kyū** for nine in order to avoid confusion.

Time

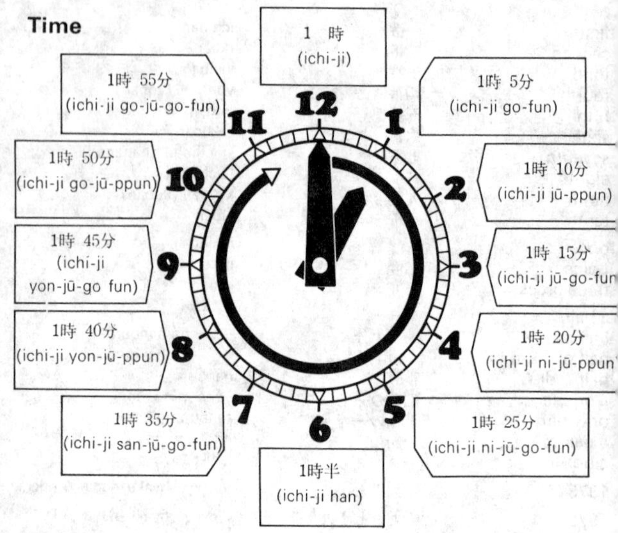

What time is it?	今何時ですか。	ima nanji desu ka
Excuse me. Can you tell me the time?	先礼ですが，今何時ですか。	shitsurei desu ga ima nanji desu ka
I'll meet you at . . . tomorrow.	明日…にお会いしましょう。	asu . . . ni o-ai shimashō
I am so sorry I'm late.	遅くなって済みません。	osoku natte sumimasen
after	過ぎ	sugi
before	前	mae
early	早い	hayai
in time	丁度間に合って	chōdo maniatte
late	遅い	osoi
midday (noon)	正午	shōgo
midnight	午前零時	gozen rēji

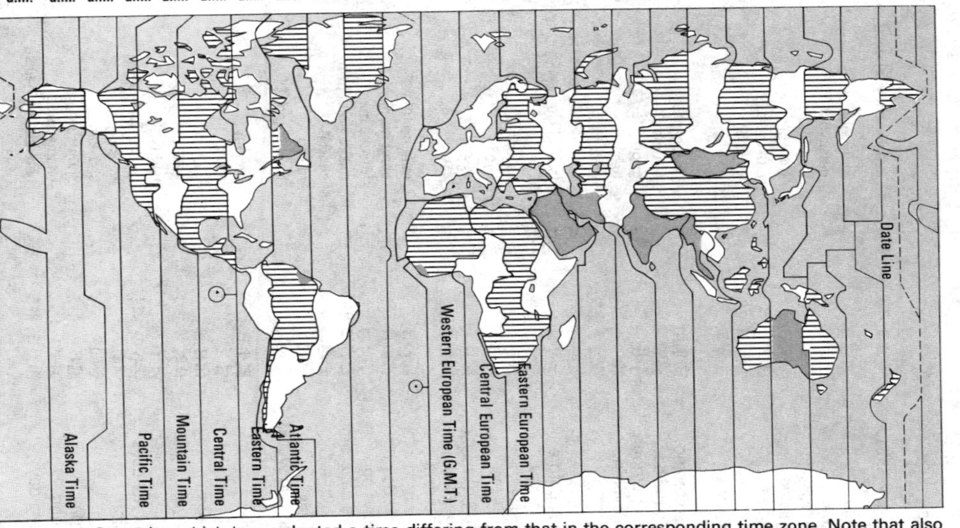

Countries which have adopted a time differing from that in the corresponding time zone. Note that also in the USSR, official time is one hour ahead of the time in each corresponding time zone. In summer, numerous countries advance time one hour ahead of standard time.

Days

What day is it today?	今日は何曜日ですか。	kyō wa nanyōbi desu ka
Sunday	日曜日	nichiyōbi
Monday	月曜日	getsuyōbi
Tuesday	火曜日	kayōbi
Wednesday	水曜日	suiyōbi
Thursday	木曜日	mokuyōbi
Friday	金曜日	kinyōbi
Saturday	土曜日	doyōbi
in the morning	午前中	gozen-chū
during the day	昼間	hiruma
in the afternoon	午後	gogo
in the evening	晩	ban
at night	夜	yoru
the day before yesterday	一昨日	issakujitsu
yesterday	昨日	sakujitsu
today	今日	kyō
tomorrow	明日	asu
the day after tomorrow	明後日	asatte
the day before	前の日	mae no hi
the next day	次の日	tsugi no hi
two days ago	二日前	futsuka mae
in three days' time	三日の内に	mikka no uchi ni
last week	先週	senshū
next week	来週	raishū
during two weeks	二週間	ni-shū kan
birthday	誕生日	tanjōbi
day	日	hi
holiday	休日	kyūjitsu
holidays	休暇	kyūka
month	月	tsuki
school holidays	学校の休暇	gakkō no kyūka
vacation	休暇	kyūka
week	週間	shū kan
weekday	週日	shūjitsu
weekend	週末	shūmatsu
working day	働く日, 平日	hataraku hi, hējitsu

Months

The Japanese calendar virtually corresponds to our Gregorian calendar. However, a new era is proclaimed with the ascension of each new emperor to the imperial Japanese throne so that years are counted according to the number of years in the reign of the emperor. Therefore, with the enthronization of Hirohito in 1926, the Showa era was proclaimed. Thus, our year 1982, for instance, would be the 57th year of Showa.

In Japanese, months are literally called first month, second month, third month, etc., which corresponds to our January, February, March. Although the Japanese calendar ist the nation's official one, days and dates are sure to be written in a Western style for Occidental travellers.

January	一月	ichigatsu
February	二月	nigatsu
March	三月	sangatsu
April	四月	shigatsu
May	五月	gogatsu
June	六月	rokugatsu
July	七月	shichigastu
August	八月	hachigatsu
September	九月	kugatsu
October	十月	jūgatsu
November	十一月	jū-ichigatsu
December	十二月	jū-nigatsu
since June	六月から	rokugatsu kara
during the month of August	八月の間	hachigatsu no aida
last month	先月	sengetsu
next month	来月	raigetsu
the month before	その前の月	sono mae no tsuki
the next month	その後の月	sono ato no tsuki
July 1	七月一日	shichigatsu tsuitachi
March 17	三月十七日	sangatsu jū-shichi-nichi

Letter headings are written thus:

Tokyo, August 17, 1973	東京にて 1973年 8月 17日
Osaka, July 1, 1973	大阪にて 1973年 7月 1日

Seasons

spring	春	haru
summer	夏	natsu
autumn	秋	aki
winter	冬	fuyu
in spring	春に	haru ni
during the summer	夏の間	natsu no aida
in autumn	秋に	aki ni
during the winter	冬の間	fuyu no aida

Public holidays

The following list isn't complete. We have noted only the most important public holidays celebrated in Japan. On most of these, banks, offices, shops and stores are closed.

January 1	New Year's Day
January 2 to 4	National Bank Holidays
January 15	Adults' Day
February 11	National Foundation Day
March 20 or 21	vernal equinox
April 29	Emperor's Birthday
May 3	Constitution Day
May 5	Children's Day
September 15	Old People's Day
September 23	autumnal equinox
October 10	National Sports Day
November 3	National Culture Day
November 23	Labour-Thanksgiving Day

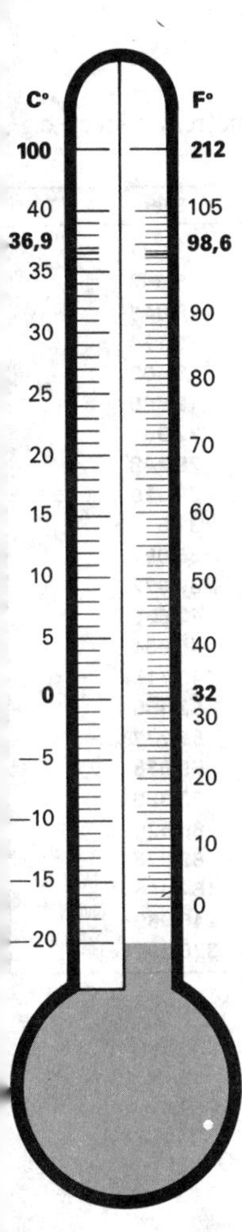

Conversion tables

To change centimetres into inches, multiply by .39.

To change inches into centimetres, multiply by 2.54.

Centimeters and inches

	in.	feet	yards
1 mm	0,039	0,003	0,001
1 cm	0,39	0,03	0,01
1 dm	3,94	0,32	0,10
1 m	39,40	3,28	1,09

	mm	cm	m
1 in.	25,4	2,54	0,025
1 ft.	304,8	30,48	0,304
1 yd.	914,4	91,44	0,914

(32 metres = 35 yards)

Temperature

To convert Centigrade into degrees Fahrenheit, multiply Centigrade by 1.8 and add 32.

To convert degrees Fahrenheit into Centigrade, subtract 32 from Fahrenheit and divide by 1.8.

REFERENCE SECTION

Metres and feet

The figure in the middle stands for both metres and feet, e.g., 1 metre = 3,281 ft. and 1 foot = 0,30 m.

Metres		Feet
0.30	1	3.281
0.61	2	6.563
0.91	3	9.843
1.22	4	13.124
1.52	5	16.403
1.83	6	19.686
2.13	7	22.967
2.44	8	26.248
2.74	9	29.529
3.05	10	32.810
3.35	11	36.091
3.66	12	39.372
3.96	13	42.635
4.27	14	45.934
4.57	15	49.215
4.88	16	52.496
5.18	17	55.777
5.49	18	59.058
5.79	19	62.339
6.10	20	65.620
7.62	25	82.023
15.24	50	164.046
22.86	75	246.069
30.48	100	328.092

Other conversion charts

For	see page
Clothing sizes	113
Currency converter	136
Customs allowances	23
Distance (miles-kilometres)	144
Fluid measures	142
Tire pressure	143

Weight conversion

The figure in the middle stands for both kilograms and pounds, e.g., 1 kilogram = 2.205 lb. and 1 pound = 0.45 kilograms.

Kilograms (kg.)		Avoirdupois pounds
0.45	1	2.205
0.90	2	4.405
1.35	3	6.614
1.80	4	8.818
2.25	5	11.023
2.70	6	13.227
3.15	7	15.432
3.60	8	17.636
4.05	9	19.840
4.50	10	22.045
6.75	15	33.068
9.00	20	44.889
11.25	25	55.113
22.50	50	110.225
33.75	75	165.338
45.00	100	220.450

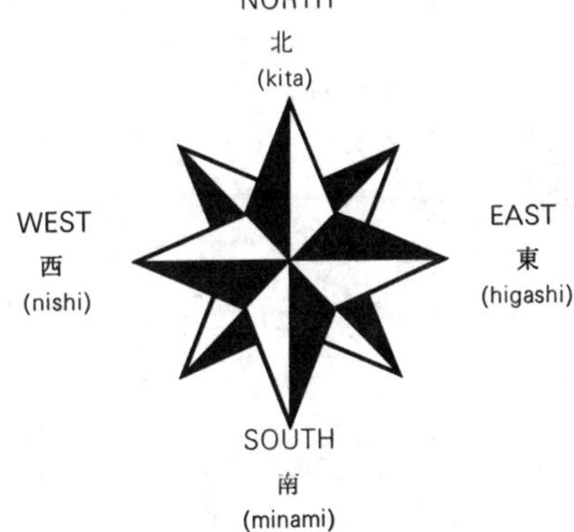

The year round . . .

Here are the average temperatures for some Japanese cities (in Fahrenheit degrees).

	Tokyo	Sapporo	Kagoshima	Osaka
January	38.7	23.1	43.9	41.7
February	39.7	23.5	45.9	42.7
March	45.7	30.2	51.4	48.7
April	55.6	42.3	59.2	58.6
May	63.7	52.3	66.2	66.0
June	70.0	60.0	72.7	72.0
July	77.2	68.0	80.2	80.2
August	79.5	71.1	80.8	80.8
September	73.0	62.2	75.9	75.1
October	62.0	50.7	66.0	64.0
November	52.3	38.5	57.2	55.3
December	43.0	27.3	48.2	46.0

What does that sign mean?

You may encounter some of the following signs or notices on your trip through Japan:

空き	Vacant
熱い	Hot
ベルを押して下さい	Please ring
注意	Caution
男子用	Gentlemen
出口	Exit
エレベーター	Lift (elevator)
閉店	Closed
非常口	Emergency exit
婦人用	Ladies
引く	Pull
触れるべからず	Don't touch
案内所	Information
犬に注意	Beware of the dog
入口	Entrance
勘定係	Cashier's
貸します	To let, for hire
警告	Warning
危険	Danger
禁煙	No smoking
…禁止	. . . forbidden
ノックせずにお入り下さい	Enter without knocking
入場禁止	No entrance
入場お断わり	No admittance
押す	Push
大売り出し	Sales
死の危険	Danger of death
私有地	Private property
使用中	Occupied
立入禁止	Keep out
止まれ	Stop
釣禁止	No fishing
冷たい	Cold
売り切れ	Sold out
売ります	For sale
予約済	Reserved

Emergency!

By the time the emergency is upon you it's too late to turn to this page to find the Japanese for "I'll scream if you. . . ". So have a look at this short list beforehand—and, if you want to be on the safe side, learn the expressions shown in capitals.

Be quick	早く	hayaku
Call the police	警察を呼んで下さい	keisatsu o yonde kudasai
CAREFUL	注意	chūi
Come here	ここに来て下さい	koko ni kite kudasai
Danger	危険	kiken
Fire	火事	kaji
Gas	ガス	gasu
Get a doctor	医者を呼んで下さい	isha o yonde kudasai
Go away	あっちに行って下さい	atchi ni itte kudasai
HELP	助けて	tasukete
Get help quickly	すぐに助けを呼んで下さい	sugu ni tasuke o yonde kudasai
I'm ill	病気です	byōki desu
I'm lost	道に迷いました	michi ni mayoimashita
I've lost my . . .	…をなくしました	. . . o nakushimashita
Leave me alone	構わないで下さい	kamawanai de kudasai
Lie down	横になって下さい	yoko ni natte kudasai
Listen	聞いて下さい	kiite kudasai
Listen to me	聞いて下さい	kiite kudasai
Look	見て下さい	mitekudasai
LOOK OUT	気を付けなさい	ki o tsuke nasai
POLICE	警察	keisatsu
Stop	止って下さい	tomatte kudasai
Stop here	ここで止まって下さい	koko de tomatte kudasai
Stop that man	あの男をつかまえて下さい	ano otoko o tsukamaete kudasai
STOP THIEF	泥棒をつかまえて下さい	dorobō o tsukamaete kudasai
Stop or I'll scream	止めないと大きな声を出しますよ	yamenai to ōkina koe o dashimasu yo

FOR CAR ACCIDENTS, see page 149

Emergency numbers

Ambulance ....

Fire ....

Police ....

Fill in these as well

Embassy ....

Consulate ....

Taxi ....

Airport information ....

Travel agent ....

Hotel ....

Restaurant ....

Babysitter ....

....

....

....

....

....

....

....

....

Index

Quick reference page

Please.	どうぞ。	dōzo
Thank you.	ありがとう。	arigato
Yes/no.	はい／いいえ。	hai/iie
Excuse me.	失礼します。	shitsurei shimasu
Waiter, please.	給仕さん，ちょっと。	kyūji san chotto
How much is that?	いくらですか。	ikura desu ka
Where are the toilets?	手洗はどこですか。	te-arai wa doko desu ka

手洗 (te-arai)	Toilets
男子用 (danshi-yō)	女子用 (joshi-yō)

Could you tell me . . . ?	…か教えて下さい。	. . . ka oshiete kudasai
where/when/why	どこ／いつ／何故	doko/itsu/naze
Help me, please.	助けて下さい。	tasukete kudasai
What time is it?	今何時ですか。	ima nanji desu ka
one/first two/second three/third	一／一番 二／二番 三／三番	ichi/ichiban ni/niban san/sanban
What does this mean? I don't understand.	これはどう言う意味ですか。分かりません。	kore wa dō yū imi desu ka. wakarimasen
Do you speak English?	英語を話しますか。	eigo o hanashimasu ka